W9-CKV-437

ADVANCED BOOK REVIEWS

"Awesome job on the book. You will definitely help many women and give them hope." —Survivor

"I can never truly understand what it could be like to experience the kind of abuse the author endured, but this book has helped me appreciate her strength and courage even more—you see, Cyndie's a member of my work team. Everyone who works with anyone should read this book. This book helped raise my awareness of the warning signs of abuse and how I may be able to help." —MaryLou, Communications Director

"Cyndie's story and words of encouragement are simply profound. She talks about horror and hope from cover to cover." —Pat, Survivor

"After reading each affirmation, I felt your courage, strength and passion grow stronger! This book validates the power of the inner spirit and soul. It is truly inspiring." —AnnMarie

"Reading your book was the first step in my own recovery. Thank you so much for having the courage, poise and strength to share your most painful stories in order to help others find a path home. You are remarkable and give others hope in knowing there is a light at the end of the tunnel." —Diane, Survivor

"Just wanted to comment that the book is great. Unfortunately your experience WAS NOT, but it will help thousands of people in similar situations, especially since you included help numbers." —Marilyn

ALSO BY THE AUTHOR

Domestic Violence Seminars

"Unchain Yourself from Domestic Violence"
"The 60-Second Difference for Police Officers"
"Recognizing Abuse in Teenage Relationships"

Cynthia Ford has developed three unique domestic violence intervention and prevention seminars that she presents to corporations, community groups, schools and police departments throughout the country.

Cynthia clarifies common misconceptions, presents statistics and facts. She illustrates how people can find help for themselves, a co-worker, family member or friend. Cynthia uses her personal experience to engage her audience and leaves them with a wealth of information.

For more information about having Cynthia speak at your company, high school, college or organization, visit **www.doorwaystofreedom.com** or write to *Doorways to Freedom, A Resource for Advocates and Survivors of Domestic Violence*, P.O. Box 403 Kearny, New Jersey 07032-0403 or call (201) 998-5929.

SEMINAR REVIEWS

"Your workshop, supported by your very approachable style, creates a safe environment in which our employees can explore very difficult issues. I strongly believe that your presence has helped people."
— Terry Ginder, CSW, CEAP, EAP Manager

"Your program has a lot of merit. We would be interested in continuing our effort to alert and educate employees to the dangers of domestic violence."
— James S. Gray, NJ Board of Public Utilities

"This class was very informative. It provided me with a better understanding of the victims and their circumstances." — Carla

"Cynthia's presentation was thought-provoking and heart warming. I'll also keep the reference materials at my desk." — Sue

"Thanks so much for giving the domestic violence seminar. It gives me a great sense of hope seeing someone like you turn their life around." — Patricia

"Thank you for baring your soul in your seminar. I admire and respect you immensely, even though I really don't know you. I think this will help many women in your situation to do something about it. I'm proud to say you are a Prudential associate." — Steve

"I've never been in an abusive relationship, but I hope to some day be able to do what you've done to bring hope to so many." — Tina

Doorways to Freedom

Cynthia Ford

All rights reserved.
Copyright © 2000 by Cynthia Ford

No part of this book may be reproduced or transmitted in any form or by any means, electronic or mechanical, including photocopying, recording or by any information storage and retrieval system, without permission in writing from the author, Cynthia Ford.

Cover design and page layout by Cynthia Ford, with assistance from Karen Cardet, Milly Figueroa, and Jeffrey Breedlove

Copyright © 1999 photo by Bruce Wodder

ATTENTION: SCHOOLS AND CORPORATIONS
Doorways to Freedom is available at quantity discounts with bulk purchase for educational, business or sales promotional use. For information, please write to: Cynthia Ford, Doorways to Freedom Inc., P.O. Box 403, Kearny, New Jersey 07032-0403, or call (201) 998-5929.

www.doorwaystofreedom.com

PRINTED IN THE UNITED STATES OF AMERICA

ISBN 0-9709480-0-X

This book is dedicated to survivors of domestic violence everywhere. May the millions of women and children who suffer each year at the hands of their loved ones break free of the violence that binds them.

I'd especially like to thank my family and friends for their unconditional love and support, my three beautiful sons, Blaine, Derek and Travis, my wonderful therapist Roseanna Zoubek and Frank, who has struggled with me.

A special thanks to Ken Dolan-Del Vecchio and Prudential for acknowledging the seriousness of domestic violence and allowing me the opportunity to present my seminar at various locations to hundreds of Prudential associates.

ACKNOWLEDGMENTS

There are so many other wonderful people who deserve recognition for the completion of this book, and I'd like to thank them from the bottom of my heart.

Robyn Kurdek
Kimberley Goode
Leigh Manganaro
Karen Cardet
Marilyn and Frank Pozzuto
Sharon Carfagna
Perry and Beth Stein
Ruth Hiatt
Karen Tildsley
Hillarie Scannelli
Glenn Nutting and Bruce Wodder
Terry Ginder
Gretchen Walsh and Lucille Grey
Joanne McCarthy
Laura McGowan
Gail Crawford

Contents

A common story, but one not often spoken.

While this may sound surprising, I have no regrets about being involved in an abusive relationship. There is no time in my life for regrets instead, there is only room for knowledge, education, experience and growth. If I wallow in regrets and self pity, then I would be no good to myself or those around me. I am not saying that I like to be treated unkindly or disrespectfully, only that I am proud to have survived my domestic violence relationship. I am also proud that I have the fortitude to share my ordeals with you, and hopefully may help you end your own ordeal.

Having survived such a terrible time in my life, I am certain that I have the strength to face anything the future has to offer. I am only more knowledgeable for having gone through many years of my life living with domestic violence. I've learned that I could free myself from domestic violence in my own time and that I was always exactly where I was supposed to be. Those many years were a time that I could not have lived any other way. I had to go through that pain and suffering in order to emerge the strong woman I am today.

Each time I was beaten, I changed. I became a different woman after my beatings. After he ridiculed me, tormented my inner soul and took advantage of my kindness, I lost a little part of who I was. I can accept that over time people change. That in time, we grow, we learn, and when we go through life's experiences we become wiser people. But when we are beaten down repeatedly, we change in another way. Sometimes in a way that is unexplainable. When we could be trusting others, we turn away from them. When we could be giving love to our loved ones, we find it difficult to express our feelings. When we could be living free from violence, we shudder at the thought of our abuser coming home, a home from which he has stolen the heart.

The abusive journey begins...Age 15, March 1984.

A teen's story: At fifteen she met her abuser. She did not know it then, but she would marry this man who would emotionally and physically abuse her for more than a decade. She did not like him at first. She avoided his phone calls. She told her girlfriends to tell him she wasn't home or she was sick, just so she wouldn't have to talk to him. But with his persistence, his gifts, his complimenting words, she began to change her mind. She began to fall in love with him. She decided he must like her, since he wanted to be with her all the time. And, of course, since he was jealous of her being with anyone but him, how could he not in fact like her?

Six months into their relationship, he hit her for the first time. She can't remember all the details, but afterwards he apologized and told her he would never do it again. If she knew that would only be the beginning of years of punches, kicks, hair-pulling and head-butting, as well as degrading verbal abuse, she would have ended their relationship that very night. Or would she have? She was the type of girl who trusted people and believed people can change. A girl who loved to do things for those in need and who would give her life to save another. After all, she believed she would save him from his personal problems. I know so much about this fifteen-year-old girl because I am that girl.

Summer 1985.

We are at a 50s dance. He reaches out to grab me and misses. I tell him not to be jealous. I tell him I love him. I tell him that I didn't look at the guy across the dance floor. I tell him to stop twisting my arm, for it hurts. His hold on me tightens and he twists it more. Everyone around us is oblivious to the pain and mental abuse he is inflicting on me. As he lets go, he instructs me not to talk or look at any other man, then he flashes me "his look." The look that means he is going to finish what he started later on tonight, no matter how I act.

I go to the bathroom to fix my make-up to hide the few tears I shed. In the bathroom I decide to leave the dance. Thinking I can escape him tonight, I walk out of the dance hall. Running to get a head start, I turn and see him running after me. I run and run and run. He catches me and pushes me to the ground. He kicks me. He pulls my long brown hair out of my head as he drags me across the concrete sidewalk. I beg him. I plead with him to stop. I cry for someone to help me, but no one hears my desperate cries. As I rise from the ground, he punches me. He says nasty words to me, and then he lets me walk home alone.

He told me that by hitting me and acting jealous he was looking out for my best interest. But in reality, it was his interest, not mine, that concerned him. I am only a possession. He thought that since I accepted his violent behavior I must have loved him.

Age 18: Spring of 1986.

Kicking me out of his car after he slapped me around and nearly tore my pants off my body was only the beginning. He drove away, leaving me in a place I did not know. I walked crying, bleeding, not knowing where I was. Then came the sound of a speeding car. I knew. I began to run. I began to run as fast as I could. My running got me nowhere. I felt like a cartoon character running in place, never getting anywhere.

When I looked back, he was in sight. He drove alongside me calling me a slut, whore, bitch and told me it was my fault that he hurt me. He said it was for my own good that he gave me a beating. He laughed as he made fun of my torn clothes.

But I got back in the car. His arm slowly went around my neck. He pulled me closer to him and told me he was sorry. He told me he loved me and did not mean to call me those words. He told me he would never do it again. That abusive event in my life was before I married him. I believed that if I couldn't run from his abuse that night, I could never run from it.

Age 19 to 25: Our living together years from 1987 to May 1993.

How many lonely nights would I cry because my abuser didn't come home? When he did, the fear that rose inside me was unbelievable. The loneliness I felt as he was unlocking the door is indescribable. I knew, even when I pretended to be asleep, I would take "a beating" or be verbally abused. Verbal abuse is painful. Sometimes I wished my abuser would hit me instead of cutting me with his nasty words. Words can be cruel. Words can cut deep. Words are powerful tools if you allow them to be. I allowed him to mentally abuse me with his words.

He would call me a whore or bitch because I put make-up on. He would ask me so many questions if I curled my hair or put on a shirt and didn't button the top button. "Why are you wearing that?" he would demand. Forget it if I looked at another man, even a man who was waiting on me at a store. It got to the point that even when I wasn't with my abuser, I would be too afraid to look at a man or not have all the buttons fastened on my shirt. How controlling he was. And how his abuse and control tore me down.

After he stayed out all night.

It's that time again. Beating time. Sunday morning, when the cocaine runs out and the beer's all gone, he stumbles home.

"Wake up you bitch, move over!" He did not have to tell me to wake up because I never went to sleep. I was absorbed with anxiety and fear since he left. He fights with me even when I stay lying down. He cusses at me, then kicks me in the back until I fall off the bed. He gets up and lies next to me on the floor. He starts saying disgusting words in my ear. He wants to have sex with me, and of course, I refuse. This only makes him more mad. He grabs my hair and drags me across the floor. I cry and plead with him to stop. He lifts me up by my hair and without notice, head butts me, knocking me down again. He leaves me on the floor and goes inside to sleep on the couch.

Ashamed. Embarrassed. Withdrawn. Untrusting. Afraid. Guilty. Fearful. Never to be clean again. I feel I can not scrub the filth away after he beats me. Water does wash away the blood, but not the bruises or scratches. My body aches from the abusive words he lashes at me like a whip. Mental abuse also makes me feel dirty. How dirty I feel just saying these last few sentences, knowing that he hurt me again.

Age 19: A day in the life of an abused woman.

Yes, it really was that bad! I curled up on the floor hoping he would just vanish. Bleeding, angry, fearful, alone, I lay there. Sobbing until he leaves the room. Staring at the wall and seeing nothing but despair. Breathing heavily, I calm myself only to hear him laughing. He makes rude comments. I do not move until I am sure he is sleeping. Using the bed to steady myself, I stand. I'm dizzy from having clumps of hair pulled out of my head. I sit on the edge of the bed, my legs shake as I stand to look in the mirror. I've been through this before and only want to cover the bruises. I don't think of myself. I think about what everyone will say when they see me.

I have to dream up excuses for this time so they are different. I also want to apologize to my abuser. Say sorry for him beating me. Say sorry for standing up to him. Tell him that everything is okay and that I believe he loves me. I know his words already. I know that he will beg my forgiveness and tell me he did not mean to hit me. Tell me he loves me. I question his love.

As I wash away the blood, I wash the experience away, too. Maybe I will not have to go out. Maybe I will not see anyone I know. Maybe I can cover the marks long enough for them to fade. Maybe no one will ever know…

…but Cynthia knows.

Age 20: Raped December 1988.

Just the thought of the word rape scares me. I told my husband he had to leave after the holidays, and he became more angry and that "look" of the devil in his eyes seemed to never leave his face. (My heart beats faster just trying to write down my thoughts.) For the first time in many years, I went to a company holiday party without him. He stayed home with our son instead of coming. Going out alone was new to me. The entire evening was spent thinking about what would happen to me when I got home. Never did I imagine I would be severely beaten and raped by my husband who was supposed to love and cherish me. Never did I think I would be so abused. So hurt. So afraid. So fearful for my life.

At the party…My husband called numerous times to find out when I was coming home. He even harassed some of my co-workers over the phone. I took a few of his calls and then decided (for the very first time in our relationship) not to take his abusive phone calls anymore. I was drinking alcohol that night, even though I was only 20. When the party was over, a few friends drove me home. Out of fear, I asked them to walk me inside so they could tell my husband I was "a good girl" and that I was sorry for not coming home sooner. How afraid I became on the ride home. I was so afraid that I can actually feel some of that fear welling up inside of me now!

I can remember being raped like it happened yesterday. My stomach turns at the thought. He gave me my worst beating that night too. How I cried! Screamed out in anger. In fear. In pain. In need of someone's help. If only they heard my screams. How humiliated I was! How cold were the police officers to me! How disgusting was the bathroom in the hospital they took me to. How the doctor looked at me when he was taking my pubic hair samples. How the nurse hurt me as she took blood from my left arm.

These details may not sound of real importance, but they will last a lifetime in my head. A lifetime. How long is his sentence? How long could it be when I was talked out of pressing charges by the detectives, especially the female officer? She told me that rape is hard to prove when it happens between a husband and a wife even with all my bruises, cuts, blood and the samples they took at the hospital. Then why did they let me go through those disgusting and embarrassing tests? I could have been home sleeping. I could have been lying in the dark with myself, instead of with those strangers. Strangers that could not have cared less what happened to me or the violence that was instilled upon me. They would have done me more justice if they told me to go home and get some sleep. Instead, they took pictures of my face and made me answer questions for hours.

Do I sound bitter? Is there sarcasm in my words? Of course, why wouldn't there be? I am still suffering. All women who have been sexually abused have the right to feel betrayed. To feel pain. To feel cast aside by others who look at them with "that look." But for today, I must learn to live with my decision of not pressing charges. I must begin to forgive myself for something that I had no control over.

Feelings of shame enter my mind. Feelings of disgust so strong I want to scrub my body until I bleed. Sound too harsh? I think not. I know I can never cleanse myself after being raped by my husband. Even if God himself came down upon me, dousing me with holy water, the memories of my rape would still linger inside me. His cleansing may wash my outer shell, but what being raped has done to me mentally will remain with me forever.

Forever. Forever is a scary thought. Over ten years have passed since I was raped. Just the thought of that night instills fear in me. An event that took only about an hour of my life that night in reality took a piece of my remaining years on this earth. Does that sound dramatic? Do these words explain how I truly feel? I don't think I can ever fully explain to you or anyone what happened to me on that December night. I can only try my best to convey the sadness, loneliness, fear, anger, hatred, confusion and pain I still suffer.

Age 21: May 1989.

How humiliating is it that we got back together after he did the most terrible thing he could do to me? Well, let me tell you — very. Why did I reconcile with the man I married after he hurt me on the outside and on the inside of my body?

Was I crazy? What was going through my thick skull? So many feelings. So many fears. So many reasons. I thought he needed me. I couldn't leave him. The guilt overpowered my fears and my angry feelings. I just shut off my feelings about that horrible night altogether. Why feel at all, I thought. Or maybe I just wasn't thinking. Maybe I wanted to "fix" our relationship, whatever the personal costs were.

Whatever my reasons were to get back with my husband, I did go back to him. I didn't go through with any of the domestic violence charges. Of course, things were never the same between us. I often think about that disgusting night. I haven't talked much about it. I'm not ashamed, but it is painful. What has helped me through these painful flashbacks is telling myself I made the best choices for me at that time in my life.

Age 22: Began working part-time for Prudential, December 1990.

Birthdays, anniversaries, holidays and the days I was abused stay in my mind for many reasons. The Superbowl reminds me of unhappy times. A time of bruises and stitches. A day to celebrate was a day to mourn. Sitting in the hospital emergency waiting room with my dad makes me sad. I was crying and struggling to compose myself. I told my dad, I could not press charges against my husband for beating me. Despite all the pain and suffering, I still couldn't bring myself to press charges. I was not ready physically or mentally to leave yet, so I went back to my prison cell.

Who understands me? Only a few...

Walk in my shoes for only a day,
Run in my shoes because there's hell to pay.
You'll pay with a put-down, punch or a kick,
The feelings of loneliness will make you so sick.
Miles and miles you'll walk in my shoes,
Miles of pain, suffering and feeling the blues.
Walking and crying and feeling like dying,
Will you walk in my shoes and keep trying?

Age 23: September 1991.

After years of physical, mental, financial and sexual abuse, my self-confidence, my courage and my outlook on my situation decreased. I was at a point in my life where I trusted no one. I questioned my faith in God. I believed that God had punished me for something I did in a previous life. My most frequently asked question to God was, "Why me?"

In September 1991, with the support of Prudential's Employee Assistance Program, I found the help I so desperately needed to begin my recovery process. I received counseling through this confidential program. It showed me the way to other women who were in similar situations. I began attending support groups and domestic violence workshops.

In time, my self-esteem grew. I started accepting me for me and my situation for what it really was. I didn't have to like it, but knew I had to accept it.

Age 25: May 1993.

The police told my abuser to leave on May 17, 1993, after I filed a temporary restraining order. My children were only six, three and one at the time. I didn't feel I had any choice but to have him ordered to leave. He would not leave voluntarily. He would never leave when I asked him. It took a lot of courage and strength for me to go to court with three young children, wait all day to see the judge, then call the police and have them make him leave. It was one on the toughest decisions I've made in my life. The fears and confusion I felt made me cry. I cried when he left. I cried when he called. I cried when I held my three children and told them their daddy was not going to live with us any more. It was okay for me to cry. What wasn't okay was for me to take him back. I endured enough pain from this person. He had caused me plenty of suffering and sadness in my life. Enough was enough! I had finally hit bottom.

Enough was enough when I put my well-being ahead of his. Enough was enough when I allowed reality back into my life. Enough was enough when I told myself I could make it without him. Enough was enough when I set boundaries for myself and did not extend them for any reason. Enough was enough when I realized I loved myself. I hadn't loved myself in so many years that it was strange at first, but then felt good.

Age 25: 1993.

Society places much of the responsibility for domestic violence on women. My experience with the justice system and the police was tiring and frustrating. I once said to an assistant prosecutor, "Am I not the victim? The abuser gets more justice then I do!" Her response, (yes, a female prosecutor said this) "This is a vicious cycle with these types of men. Keep changing your phone number, have your kids call from a pay phone so your ex-husband can't get your number. We can't put a police officer outside your door." She and other employees of the justice system sometimes make battered women feel like their lives are worthless. They are often too quick to blame the victim. Some of them will tell you they are overworked and underpaid. They leave out that they chose their profession in justice so they could help people and give something back to their communities.

Another assistant prosecutor (a man this time) told me, "This is a burnt-out job." They can't comprehend that abused women are burned out too. How many complaints did I file over the years? Probably too many to count. Nevertheless, I deserve as much time and consideration as other victims. I pay taxes. I am a human being who deserves to be treated with dignity and respect. They are too quick to judge abused women. Stress in a day of an abused woman's life is a month in the life of a person who is not abused. Just because I know my abuser doesn't give the courts the right to make me feel like I'm the bad guy or that my justice is less deserving!

When I finally made up my mind to follow through with domestic violence charges against my husband, I knew I was changing. Never in my life had I gone through with any of these charges. Never had I stood up for Cynthia. It was time to move on in my life. Time to live my life.

I made four domestic violence charges against him. I couldn't stop my anxiety attacks or my legs from shaking, but I made it through his plea bargaining (three years' probation and 30 days in jail). He made an open apology to me in court. I never accepted it. I have much anger towards him, but I am moving on.

I have three beautiful, healthy children and a wonderful and challenging career. And I have friends for the very first time in my life.

Age 26: Divorced ten years to the day that my abuser and I started dating.

The months ahead were very difficult for me. I was with my three young children without my husband for the first time. Or was I? I had to do things all by myself. I didn't have him to fall back on. Or did I ever really? I realized I could never really have fallen back on him. I had been married to a non-participating partner anyway. What difference did it make for him not to be in the same house as I was? Well, to be truthful, it was finally peaceful. I enjoyed coming home. I wasn't afraid to unlock the door. All my household matters were up to me. I was the "queen of my castle," even though I lived in a five-room apartment.

Why did the man who claimed his love for me hurt me? Power. Control. The things men are taught about their place in the world and their "rights" within family life? Because of childhood problems that he carried into our marriage? Because of his alcohol and drug abuse? Because of jealousy and lack of respect for himself and for me?

I don't need to search for more reasons. As a battered woman was once quoted within a newspaper account, "There ain't no dammed reason good enough."

What women affected by domestic violence need to accept is that even when their abuser sees the stars in the sky, he may never see the light. Even when I come to realize that domestic violence is no longer in my cards, my abuser may not change his deck. Even when I make those phone calls to get him help, drive him to rehab centers or places for men that batter, I can not do his footwork for him. I have tried to make him stop abusing me. I have begged him. I've pleaded with him. I've loved him as much as I possibly could. All these things have not changed his behavior so far, so what makes me continue to think I will eventually change him? I cannot change any adult males who abuse; it is up to them to change themselves.

When I was living with domestic violence 24 hours a day, I did not know who I was. I did not have time to know. I was always worrying about my abuser. Plagued by concerns about his next episode or his next misadventure. I did not know what I liked or disliked during the years I was abused. I knew what he liked and what would upset him. His likes and dislikes became mine. Over time, I gave my life to him without realizing it. I didn't realize that he controlled my every move. I didn't realize how his abuse required me to give up so much in order to merely survive.

Age 32: The new me.

I am no longer a victim of domestic violence. I have come to recognize how strong I am. I am a good person. I am scared, but I am not afraid to admit that. I have courage, even if I don't think so all the time. I have feelings, even though many days I can't feel. I get angry. I get upset. I have cried many sleepless nights. I have taken many beatings. I have been called many unacceptable words. I have needs. I have dreams. I have hopes. I am a survivor. I will survive this day. I will take this day that God has given me to better myself and my situation. Whatever I choose to do with this day, let me do one productive thing for myself; let me live today for me.

It's been many years since I began writing and publicly speaking out about domestic violence. I never imagined how much personal growth I would acquire in writing, researching and talking with thousands of women who are affected, as I have been, by an abusive partner. My book is a gift, not only to myself, but to any woman who opens it. May she learn in her own time that she is never alone.

Before you begin reading your first of 100 affirmations; thank you for letting me share a very difficult and challenging time in my life. I know that I have given you a lot to work with, but I've been through so much that I wanted to paint a clear picture of what happens in the life of a battered woman. Unfortunately, many horrible events had to be written to paint that picture. But as the saying goes, "a picture tells a thousand words."

Today, my days are filled with promise. I'm in a much better place and I am grateful for that. My three sons are 14, 11, and nine. They have a healthier mom and safer environment. They have also come a long way in the years since their father has left. We still have our difficult days dealing with issues about their father, but we're doing OK. As they say in Al Anon, "I have a lot of gratitude in my attitude."

Regards,

Cynthia

100 Affirmations

The following are intended for women of all walks of life. They were written to help past and present victims identify with feelings and emotions caused by domestic violence. Whether these readings become a daily or weekly meditation for you; take them at your own pace.

Doorways to Freedom hopes to give you a moment each day to take another step closer to freedom, whatever your definition of freedom may be.

At the bottom of each page is a dedication to a person or persons who have directly or indirectly touch the life of a battered woman.

1. UNCHAIN THE LINK

Doorways to Freedom is dedicated to all those affected by domestic violence. Whether you pick up this book today for yourself, a friend, a family member or a co-worker, I hope you will put it down with a better understanding of domestic violence. And that understanding will give you a newfound power.

Before you begin your journey to unchaining the links that bind you, let me share with you a few facts on family violence.

- Men that batter and the women and children that are abused are from all walks of life.
- Those that abuse can be rich, poor or middle-class, and can hold any type of job.
- Abusers are white, black, young, old, thin, obese, short, tall, educated, uneducated, heterosexual, gay, lesbian, bisexual, and transgender.
- Every nine seconds a woman is beaten by her partner in the United States. That's 6.7 women per minute… 400 an hour…9,600 per day…67,200 a week…and almost 4 million women a year!

These facts prove that you are not alone. By reading this page you have begun unlinking the violence that binds you.

Dedicated to my good friend, Hillarie Zoe and our similarities.

2. I Am Who I Am

I am a woman. I am a survivor and a victim of domestic violence. I am strong, no matter what others may think. I am a good person. I am scared but I am not afraid to admit that. I am someone who hurts.

I have courage, even if I do not think so all the time. I have feelings, even though many days I cannot feel. I get angry. I get upset. I have cried many sleepless nights. I have taken many beatings. I have been called many unacceptable words. I have needs. I have hopes. I have dreams.

I am a survivor. I will survive this day. I will take this day that my Higher Power has given me to better myself and my situation. Whatever I choose to do with this day, let me do one productive thing for myself. Let me live today for me.

Dedicated to those victims of domestic violence seeking the reality of their situations today.

3. DEAD BUT NOT FORGOTTEN

Today is a day to remember all the women who were murdered by their partners. In 1999, 1,218 American women died at the hands of men they once loved. That's 3.3 women a day, 23 each week and 101 a month.

By noon, one of our sisters will be killed by her partner. At 9:00 p.m., another domestic violence victim will die from wounds inflicted by the one who claimed he loved her. And just before the death clock strikes midnight on this day, one more victim will fall dead.

Let me consider this day if my life might end in the same terrifying and horrible way 3.3 other women's lives did today. I must realize that even one life taken by domestic violence in a year is too much, and someday that one life could be mine.

Let me take this day to fully absorb this information. I don't know what tomorrow holds for me.

Dedicated to Nicole and Ron who were murdered.

4. Domestic Violence

Who Are We? "Victims of domestic violence" we are labeled. "Stupid women who don't want to leave," the world gossips. Battered by their husbands or boyfriends." "She deserved to be beaten," the old man yells as she is taken away in a speeding ambulance. The paramedic laughs and says, "She's the third domestic violence victim this week we've taken to the hospital—she'll go back."

Outsiders seem to know it all. They tell you the shouldas, wouldas and couldas! What they don't know, is the pain and suffering domestic violence victims experience. We are women. Strong women. We have been living a nightmare for too long. We hurt and the hurt goes deep. It's become who we are.

We are women with low self-esteem. Women who don't trust. Women who have little boundaries. Women who want to change, but are scared. We are women who are "caught-up" in our own loneliness. It is a loneliness only other victims of domestic violence can know.

Today is a day to close our minds to criticism and open ourselves to finding support, because we deserve a life free of domestic violence.

Dedicated to The Family Violence Prevention Fund.

5. JEALOUSY AND CONTROL

Wearing white clothes, shorts, skirts, high heels, make-up, having friends, getting phone calls, eye contact with men, family, and my job are some of the things that sparked my abuser's jealousy.

No white. He hated me in white clothes. *"Men can see your bra,"* he said. *"High heels are for sluts."* He thought I only wanted attention. It didn't occur to him I wanted to look good for myself. When we look good, we feel good. And when we feel unhappy, that shows, too.

Many days I gave my abuser complete control. I never meant for this to happen; somehow it just did. Taking back control over my life was a long process. I had to take it one issue at a time, one day at a time, and finally, one link at a time.

Dedicated to Virginia in New Jersey and her fight with domestic violence.

6. Pretending Everything is Okay is Called Denial

Pretending everything is all right is not all right. Keeping a secret about being abused is not healthy. Pretending things will get better is like pretending he'll never hurt you again. Unless he gets professional help, things won't get better. Unless you get the support you need, your abusive situation may only get worse. Living in denial may be the death of you.

I was in denial for many years during my abusive relationship. Denial could have killed me. I could not pretend any longer that a prince would rescue me. I had to learn to rescue myself.

I remember saying to my brother-in-law one night when my abuser sent me to the emergency room, "I fell down the stairs. He never hit me." What a lie! I couldn't deal with the pain my abuser inflicted on me. I couldn't face the fact that my husband could beat me and still say he loved me. I wasn't ready to deal with those painful feelings. It was one thing to tend to my physical scars, but the emotional scars were another story.

Denial means not facing the truth. Denial means pretending, so you don't feel. Denial means, not having to change. To deny the truth is an injustice to yourself. To deny your right to an abuse-free life is to give up hope, and without hope there is nothing.

Dedicated to Kathleen D., who was murdered by her boyfriend.

7. RAPE

Rape is an act of violence. Rape is one of the most devastating events in a woman's life. It can destroy her. It changes who she is forever! I know. I was raped.

Rape means hate. Rape means power. Rape means control. Rape, it means many sick things to the one who commits it. I was raped by my husband at age 20. Years later, I am finally dealing with it.

You are not alone if you've been raped by your husband or boyfriend. It is estimated that more than one million American women are raped one or more times every year by their husbands.

If you are still with the person who raped you, stay strong. Get help to deal with your emotions. I stayed with my abuser for four years after the rape. Don't hate yourself for staying. Don't punish yourself for not pressing charges. It is very difficult to prove you were raped by your husband, and the laws vary state to state.

Remember, it is not your fault. When you say, "NO" it means no. Rape may not hear you but hear yourself and your cries for help. You can get the help you deserve!

Dedicated to the estimated one million American women raped by their husbands each year.

Rape and Run

I ran up the stairs to get away, and my abuser ran,
for he had his lay. My face was dripping with blood so red,
I genuinely wished, that I was dead.
But death did come, to a part of me that night,
being raped by my husband instilled in me, such fright.
He tied up my hands as I begged him to stop,
then pulled up my dress and got up on top.
I cringe at the thought to tell you the rest,
but I must finish this page, it is for the best.
He punched in my face as he stuck in his dick,
my stomach now turns, just the thought makes me sick.
His laugh I remember, his eyes oh so dark,
he beat me, he raped me, he left me his mark.
He thought I would stay and just lay on the floor,
my plans were much different, for I opened our door.
I started to run up the stairs to get free,
he got a hold of my dress and tore it you see.
His grip did not hold me, I had too much desire,
my husband was now a rapist, a batterer and a liar.
As I made it up the stairs, my husband ran for the door,
he knew I had him beat, I would be raped by him no more.
With the rape, the beaten, and the damage done,
My life was changed forever, because of my husband's sick fun.

8. NEVER TO BE CLEAN AGAIN

Ashamed. Embarrassed. Withdrawn. Untrusting. Afraid. Guilty. Fearful. Never to be clean again. You feel you cannot scrub the filth away after he beats you. Water washes away the blood, but not the bruises and scratches. Your mind and body ache from the abusive words he lashes at you like a whip. The mental abuse makes you feel so dirty.

Knowing that he hurt you over and over. Coming to grips with the fact that you cannot even be with another man because of the pain he has caused you. Believing you are not worthy of anyone else. Considering your body may be unattractive to another man. These feelings are embedded in your soul.

Allow yourself to cry. Cry for what he has done. Cry for doubting who you are. You can only expect so much growth in your self-confidence. You are who you are because of what has happened in the past. You may not like it, but you can learn to accept it and to deal with your feelings. Today is the day to say over and over that it's okay to feel this way. On this day, allow yourself to be okay with who you are, what you have endured, and how you feel about your history.

Dedicated to Sharon, my sister, my friend.

9. Fear, Courage, Strength

My fears kept me from having the courage to change. My fears kept me from having the strength to change. My fears didn't like change. My fears let my abuser win the battle of domestic violence. My fears allowed me to accept unacceptable behavior. My fears kept me from meeting people. My fears kept me living a lie. My fears kept me saving my abuser every time he got into trouble. My fears kept me up waiting for my abuser to come home. My fears kept me from sleep. My fears got the best of me.

When I stopped letting my fears rule my life I found I had the courage and strength to ask for help. I was able to file a restraining order against my abuser and follow through with domestic violence charges. I had fears while I was going through my divorce, but my courage was stronger, and it gained strength each day.

Let me start and end the day with the Serenity Prayer:
God grant me the serenity to accept the things
I cannot change. The courage to change the things I can.
And the wisdom to know the difference.

Dedicated to Toni and her struggles with domestic violence.

10. Shame and Disappointment

My abuser always disappointed me, so I learned not to put all of my eggs in one basket. I would try not to get my hopes up, but no matter how hard I tried, I would somehow let him get the best of me. I allowed him to disappoint me time and time again. How could I allow myself to think he'd come through for me? How could I think he wouldn't say those hurtful things to me again? How could I think he wouldn't hit me anymore?

I think it was because I loved him. I wanted him to be "normal"…whatever normal is. It's human nature to dream, and it's my right to hope. But sometimes I got caught up in my dreams. I would allow my dreams and my trust to disappoint me. Just like I had hopes that my abuser would stop hurting me, I had hopes of getting out of our relationship. Both seemed unreal to me at the time, but I still dreamed.

Finally, I made my dreams a reality. I left my abuser. The dreams of us having the perfect marriage melted, but the dreams of me living an abuse-free life began to grow.

I don't feel shame anymore. I used to believe it was my fault. Now, I am proud of who I am, and proud that I survived an abusive relationship. It's tough. It still hurts. My tunnel of abuse is behind me, but my tunnel of pain still holds me sometimes, and that's okay for today.

Keep your hopes alive today and your tomorrows will bring your dreams.

Dedicated to the Lilith Fair and its contributions to domestic violence victims.

11. Hope

As a survivor of domestic violence, I can fully understand how it feels to live a life without hope. As a woman who struggles endlessly with the effects of domestic violence, I can say only, "never give up hope." Sometimes when you are at your lowest, hope is all you have. If that's the case, when you lose the last ray of hope, you give up on finding the light to your tunnel's end. That could be devastating.

A recovery program can help your hope gain ground. Recovery is progress, not perfection. Just as our hopes and dreams need to grow, so does our recovery. Without hope you are hopeless; without a recovery plan, your life of family violence will only continue.

Don't stop hoping if you are not ready to start your recovery today. Keep your dreams alive, because life is too short to stop dreaming. Find courage and take your first steps out of your tunnel. Change is all around us, so catch it! You won't want to throw it back.

Dedicated to James and Christopher, my pals.

12. On Your Own Without Abuse

A new life may seem out of your reach, but it's not. Being out on your own may feel like an eternity away, but it's not. Living without abuse may feel impossible to you, but it's not. These three things can be yours if you want them. You have the courage and the strength to live without abuse. You just might not know it yet. You have to want to change. Once you are ready to make all the necessary changes in your life, don't look back. Keep your head up. It's common to feel guilty and sorry for your abuser. It's time you did something for you. You've been doing for him for so long that you are not used to putting yourself first. Once you take the first few steps, keep going. You may want to call him or go back to him, but think of how much you have suffered. Ask yourself these questions, "Will he change?" "Will he really never hurt me again?" "Will he stop verbally abusing me?" If you say no, or even maybe, to any of these questions, you made the right decision to start your abusive-free life.

You don't deserve to be a punching bag. You are worth more than a doormat. You are above enduring the hurtful words that are thrown at you. When you start thinking things are tough without him, think of how rough things are with him. When you are not with him and you lay your head down on your pillow — listen to how peaceful it is. Yes, you may be afraid he'll come and get you, but he's not there with you now. He's not in your face yelling at you. He's not hitting you. Remember your pain. Remember your scars. Remember your tears. Things can get better without him. Your deserve a life without abuse. You deserve no less.

Dedicated to Valerie for her guidance, love and support during my years in Al-Anon.

13. New Beginnings

It may be a day of joy for you. It may be a day of sadness. Whatever you feel on this day, or any other day of the year, remember that each day is a precious gift, and you must never give up on yourself.

This may be one of the worst months of the year. It may symbolize another year of abuse, another year of torture that you may endure. Keep trying if you have setbacks. We all have them. Keep learning from your mistakes. Take one day at a time. Don't look at your day as a failed 24 hours; look at it as another day you have survived and conquered.

No matter what stage of your life you are in, no matter how old, how young, how battered you are—there is help. You don't have to be a doormat your entire life. Take this day to start walking through your tunnel, because all tunnels are connected in some way—keep walking. Don't stop. Keep reaching for those links. If you reach out for help, you will find it.

Dedicated to Barbara for her friendship and for my new Goddaughter, Noelle Marie.

14. Leaving and Going Back

We got back together after he did the most terrible thing he could do to me. He beat and raped me. Why did I reconcile with the man I married after he hurt me that way? So many feelings. So many fears. So many reasons. I went back mainly because I thought he needed me. I couldn't leave him. The guilt overpowered my fears and my angry feelings. I just shut off my feelings about that horrible night altogether. Why feel at all I thought? Or maybe I wasn't thinking.

Whatever my reasons were for getting back with my husband, I did go back to him. I didn't press any rape or domestic violence charges. Of course, the way I viewed my husband was never the same. I often think about that disgusting night. I'm not ashamed, but it is painful. Telling myself, "*I made the best choices at that time in my life as I could*" has helped me deal with these flashbacks." For a long time I didn't have a support group or any counseling, either.

I have collected many links over the years by learning to stop being so hard on myself for the choices I made. Yes, it is hard to let go of the fact that I left my abuser, and although I had all the reasons in the world to stay away, I went back to him anyway.

Today, I am happy with my life. I am no longer with my abuser, and that freedom alone is enough to help me forgive myself for all the times I took him back. Just for this moment, it lets me be easier on myself.

Dedicated to Milly and Leo for all the support over the years.

15. Children and Violence Do Not Mix

Children are trusting souls. Children are what their environment makes them. If they see violence, they are affected by it. Children are innocent. They want the love and affection of their parents or their guardians. If they do not get that love and affection, they suffer. And how much they suffer varies from child to child.

Just for today, allow me to practice patience. If my children make me angry, give me the strength to count to 10 before deciding what to do. My children are my responsibility. Whether I'm with my own children or someone else's, give me the patience today to discipline them without violence.

Dedicated to Charline B. and her freedom from domestic violence.

16. RESPONSIBILITY

For many years of my life I took responsibility that was not mine to take. I couldn't say *"NO!"* I felt guilty, so I kept adding to my already heavy load. Why did I feel obligated to take on so much? The second of six children, I wasn't asked more than the rest. My memories of my youth are more happy than sad. I enjoyed being a kid, up until the age of fifteen. That's when I met my abuser.

I was always with him. We did everything together. We were inseparable. We did have some happy moments. Not all of our relationship was bad, but that was mostly in the early stages. After a while, his problems became my problems, and my problems were only my problems. I was always the one saving him from gloom and doom. If he needed money, I came through for him the best I could. If he needed a place to stay, I let him stay. If he wanted to punch something or curse someone out, that too was my responsibility. I was his cushion. I never meant for it to happen, it just did.

Taking responsibilities that did not belong to me not only hurt me, it hurt the person I took them from. Today let me consider if I have taken responsibilities that were not mine to take and decide if it is the right time to give them back.

Dedicated to Linda from Minnesota and Kraig from Illinois. Give them the strength they need to continue in their fight against domestic violence.

17. COMPASSION

The love I give to those who are in a similar tunnel as mine—the women affected by domestic violence—is a very unique love. They are always in my prayers and thoughts. I pray that they will find the strength to seek the help that is right for them. I have hope that they too have hope. But most of all, I am able to share experiences with those who need them the most.

Today we can practice having a bit more compassion for those around us. Even our abusers need some compassion. They are suffering, too. I'm not feeling sorry for my abuser, but if I send a little compassion his way, I will be a better person. I don't condone his abusive actions, NOT EVER, but if I can accept him for who he is, then I can better accept myself for who I am. Compassion is essential in my life, to prevent my feelings from turning to stone.

Tomorrow may be different, but just for today I will show compassion to those who need it. If I cannot show compassion to others on this day, then let me practice compassion toward the most important person in my life, the one I spend the most time with each and every day—me!

Kindness and love have their limits. Allow me to realize mine.

Dedicated to Robyn Kurdek, your ability to write and our lunches.

18. FRUSTRATION TOWARD WOMEN IN SIMILAR SITUATIONS

A friend of mine is currently in the situation I was in a few years ago. She's not being physically abused, but she is being severely mentally, verbally and financially abused by her husband. My friendship with her consists partially of sharing advice. I always finish my advice with, "the decisions are yours to make, I don't want to tell you what to do." It's frustrating waiting for her to be sick and tired of being sick and tired, but I know I cannot do her footwork for her.

I must turn my feelings of frustration and powerlessness over to my Higher Power. I can keep her in my prayers. Only she will know when she is ready to stop the abuse. She can only be where she is, not where I want her to be. If I can just be a friend to her when she needs me, that is all I can ask of myself. I cannot change her, just like I cannot change her abusive husband.

But I feel the pain for her. I cry for her. I love her and her children, and I only want what's best for all of them. These feelings are very important to our friendship. I let her know that I was there once. I let her know she is going through her tunnel at her own pace. It's progress, not perfection. She will never be alone. I will continue to be her friend!

Allowing a friend to share her feelings with you on domestic violence is helpful to both of you. Listening to another woman on this topic, helps the listener heal as much as the one who is sharing. So, today is a day for friendship.

Dedicated to Alice for her friendship and her years of pain and suffering at the hands of her husband.

19. A Past Sadness

What are the reasons for going through all the pain and suffering associated with an abusive marriage? Why do we suffer? It seems like we remember the bad more than we remember the good. The same goes for the news on television. It really should be called the "Bad News," because painful experiences sell more than happy ones.

When something goes wrong in my life, I blame him. When a dish breaks, I blame him. When my children are sick, I blame him. When I'm low on finances, I blame him. When I had a rough day at the office, I somehow wind up blaming him. I'm not with him any more, but I always say to myself, "It's his fault this happened to me. If he was here to help me, the kids wouldn't have gotten so sick. If he would send money, then I wouldn't be so strapped financially." My "if onlys" go on and on.

When I'm down on myself for all the bad things going on in my life, I need to get back to the present. When something happens in my life to bring back those terrible memories, I need to get out of the new hole I just dug for myself as quickly as possible. Living in the past will not ease my suffering. Blending present circumstances with past feelings only puts me in a more lonely state of mind. I have to remember to stay in the present today and always.

When I'm unhappy, it rubs off on those around me. If I'm happy, the people around me are happier. Just for this moment, I will smile. I will be happy.

Dedicated to Wendy who lost her sister to domestic violence.

20. LOVE, WHAT IT'S NOT

Love is not abuse.
Love is not jealous.
Love is not pain.
Love is not unkind.
Love is not revenge.
Love is not suffering.
Love doesn't hurt.
Love doesn't boast.
Love doesn't possess.
Love doesn't hit.
Love isn't disgusting.
Love isn't filth.
Love isn't power over another.
Love isn't control.
Love isn't hate.

This poem describes what love is not. An abuser doesn't give love; he gives what love is not. Knowing the difference between love and what love isn't is power in my pocket! I now have that power, and I can share it with you. Realizing what love truly is allows me to have healthy relationships. If your partner is giving you what love is not, then maybe it is time to find out what love really is.

Dedicated to Joanne and Silvia in Union, NJ.

21. Memories of Physical Abuse

When I remember our wedding day, our divorce date, his birthday and certain holidays, my stomach turns. When I pass a particular restaurant that brings back painful memories, I cry. When I see an answering machine, I cringe. My abuser hit my face with one sending me to the emergency room for stitches. After all was said and done, I felt sorry for him. I didn't press charges against him for hitting me with the machine, I felt too much guilt and shame.

His physical abuse has scarred me for life. I do my best to make it through those rough days that fill me with painful memories. I can't say I am grateful for living in an abusive relationship, but I can say that I am grateful to be alive and to have learned about domestic violence. I have gratitude in my life now. Through all my pain and suffering, I've learned a great deal. I am wiser from my domestic violence experiences. If I can help just one woman with my thoughts, then my pain and suffering was worth it. Thought for the day: Make me proud of you, make yourself proud, and get help to get out of your domestic violence situation.

Dedicated to Sharon, her daughter and grandchild for their pain from alcoholism.

22. Take Pride In Your Accomplishments

Be grateful you woke up this morning. Be proud you made it through this day. No matter how small your daily accomplishments were, they are done, and you should feel proud of them. If you had a good day, be grateful. If you are in a not-so-good place right now, be grateful you are not in a worse position.

Every step you take out of your tunnel of violence, is a step toward a healthier life. Sometimes, you may feel you are not progressing fast enough. There may be times when you take a few steps back. You will start walking proud again, probably before you realize.

Take one day at a time, even when things are going good. Take some time in your day to pat yourself on the back. Make a list of accomplishments for your day or make a list of *"things to do."* You'll feel good after you've crossed off an item on your list. Again, don't pressure yourself into finishing your *"things to do"* list. You already have a lot of responsibilities.

Most importantly, if you are not in a support group for women, or you're not seeking professional help, make that phone call. Do it today. Do it tomorrow. Do it soon. When you go to a support group meeting or a counseling session, you'll feel a sense of freedom. You'll feel proud of who you are, and this feeling will also bring you self-respect. When you gain self-respect, your life can only move forward. Be proud of yourself, today and every day.

Dedicated to all those who can feel proud they are surviving the day.

23. Verbal Abuse and Keeping My Mouth Shut

Words hurt in so many ways. Sometimes I become immune to them. Other times, the things he says to me cut me worse than a knife and the way he looks at me with his eyes will speak so loud sometimes that I have to cover my ears. Oh, the sound of his voice or the scream in his eyes can destroy me if I let them. My tears are for all the women who have been affected by someone else's painful remarks. Just like a picture can tell a thousand words, a word can tell a thousand stories.

Each of my thousand stories is similar to the next. Every time my abuser puts me down, verbally degrades me in public, laughs at me for my own opinion, or just glances at me, a part of me is destroyed. A piece of who I am is stolen. I've said many times to my abuser, "I would rather you steal material possessions from me than steal part of my soul. You've taken so much of me." He never quite understood what I meant, but if you are verbally and mentally abused, you're probably able to relate to what I went through.

When he's in my face and looking to start a fight, I will try my hardest to keep my mouth shut. Keeping my lips buttoned, enables me to keep an inner peace. I won't feed his fire with my own negative words. Let me leave the room, take a walk or simply nod my head and allow him to speak (or yell). I can physically be in the same place with him, but I can practice leaving mentally for a moment. All I can hope is that his verbal abuse will stop. Sometimes, even when I do absolutely nothing, he hits me or keeps throwing his harsh words at me. When he gets like this, let me do what I can to get out of his path.

Dedicated to Patty and her good sense of humor, even when things get tough.

24. Disappointments

When I hear the word disappointment, I automatically answer "yes." Yes, I've had many disappointments in my life. Yes, most have been a direct result of my abuser. What do I do?

First, I say to myself, "I told you so." I knew in my heart and mind that he would disappoint me again. He's done it over and over to me. My reaction varies. I may scream, cry, give the silent treatment or even take it out on my children.

Whatever my disappointments are this time, the way I handle them is my choice. By thinking things through before reacting, I can calm myself and keep my dignity. This way, I won't disappoint myself or my children. The damage of his disappointment is enough, let me not add to it.

Dedicated to Maria for what she has faced from an abuser that is also a police officer.

25. Physical Abuse

Physical abuse is on my mind today. Not that it doesn't cross my mind every day, but today it is a pressing issue. I was abused physically by my boyfriend for almost three years. I then married him. He was supposed to love and cherish me, but instead he abused me for another seven years. During my life of living in hell or what I think my hell would be, I was beaten many, many times. My blood was on his hands more than I care to remember. He pulled my hair, and the lumps on my head lingered for days. Head-butts were his specialty, I always received a few when he beat me. I share this with you because I feel compelled to. Because it is my obligation as a woman and a mother to speak the truth about my domestic violence relationship.

Looking back on this critical time in my life, I shed many tears. Tears of pain, loneliness, fear and depression. And I cried also tears of joy for the birth of my three sons. All my tears were not shed in vain. Writing this book and becoming the woman I am because of the abuse was worth those tears.

If nothing else today, let me have a good cry. To cry is healthy. Crying releases some of my pain.

Dedicated to Debbie in Hoboken, New Jersey for her role in the fight against domestic violence.

26. JUST FOR TODAY

Today I will do something for me. I will enjoy the good things in my life. I will not take tomorrow for granted. Today is a gift from my Higher Power. I will try not to focus on the negative energy. I have to take whatever good I get and expand on it. I want to enjoy my feelings of happiness for as long as I can. If nothing goes well today, then I need to take an item on the list below and make it happen. If it is not listed, then I'll fill in the blank and accomplish it. If my schedule is busy and there's no time for me, let me call a "self time-out." When I am feeling down on myself because of something my abuser did, give me the strength to replace that negativity with something positive.

Things You Can Do For You.

Read a book.	Buy something for yourself.
Take a bath.	Take a nap.
Go for a walk.	Go to a support group meeting.
Start a diet.	Volunteer.
Eat a piece of chocolate.	Hug your children.
Go to a movie.	Smile.
Take a college course.	_____ (fill in)

Dedicated to Barbara for sharing her personal stories.

27. Listening

Listening to others is a gift. Listening without passing judgement is another gift—a greater gift. Watching the body language of a woman who has been affected by domestic violence is sometimes all you need to understand her and to feel the pain she suffers. She lowers her head or looks down when she is talking, especially if her abuser is near. She covers her bruises with her hands or with clothes. Even in the summer, she may wear long sleeve clothing and pants. She has a hard time talking to men because she's usually not allowed to do so. She barely makes eye contact. She even finds it difficult to look at her abuser. This behavior is out of fear. It happens because her partner treats her like a possession. She fears because she knows what the abuse is like.

Listen to yourself repeating the same phrases over and over, "I'm gonna leave him!" "I've got to leave." "I'm gonna kill myself or kill him if he hits me again!" "Maybe he's right, I am no good." "I wish he wouldn't drink." I hope he's not doing drugs again." "I'm sorry." "It's okay." "I know you didn't mean to hurt me." "Stop calling me those names!" "Officer, I don't want to press charges." "Mom, he's not that bad." "God, why me?"

If you have said any of these phrases or anything remotely similar, you are in a violent situation and need help. You need to think about how many times you have said these things…probably too many to count.

Think about not saying them. Think about getting help and learning a new way of life. Unless he's willing to get serious professional help, he won't change. You have to take the first step. Start by telling yourself, "I want a better life." "I deserve a good life." "I am entitled to a life free of domestic violence." "I deserve no less!" So, listen to yourself today.

Dedicated to Ruth H. and Karen T. for being my friends and making me laugh.

28. TOUGH LOVE

On this day, just about every song we hear on the radio has the word "love" in it. The different artists sing about the meaning of love. They sing about what love is. They sing about lost love, making love, true love and first love. Does anyone sing about "tough love?" Tough love is the hardest love to give. It is difficult, because the one we are tough loving doesn't believe we love them. They think we are abandoning them, when really the opposite is true — we are helping them.

If we are experiencing abuse from a loved one, whether verbal or mental, sometimes we need to walk away for a while. Sometimes we need professional help to deal with what is happening to us. We may need to go away for a weekend. We may need to stay with a friend or relative. Sometimes the person who is abusing us needs professional help. They may need one-on-one counseling for domestic violence. They may need a rehabilitation center for drugs or alcohol abuse. Sometimes, jail is the only answer. Wherever you or your abuser may need to go, tough love may be unique to your situation. Today, be tough enough to give tough love. If you love something let it go. If it comes back to you, it's yours. If it doesn't, it never was.

Dedicated to Bonnie and Danny. They have always been there and I love them deeply. And to their beautiful daughter Elizabeth Ann.

29. Loneliness With a Sense of Humor

Valentine's Day. The day after the flowers and chocolates. For many American women, this day is one of self-worth, inner peace and inner happiness. For other women, it is a day of loneliness, insecurity and sadness. It's a day to think about more bad memories and disappointments.

To the women who are happy today, good for you. May your roses last more than a week, may your chocolates melt in your mouth, and may the joyful memories last a lifetime. To those of you feeling sad…smile. Look at the good in your life and there is good, if you look for it. Be grateful for what you have.

Holidays and special dates stir feelings in all of us. If we let ourselves we can get sucked into lonely feelings. It is difficult to look at the bright and positive things in our lives when we feel lonely. When we become aware of how we are feeling, then we can start to come out of our shells. Today, practice feeling grateful again. For now, let us think about what's in the day. The only thing we should be thinking of today, is all the half-price sales on Valentine's Day goodies tomorrow!

When you feel lonely, think about the things you are grateful for. When you feel sad, keep a good sense of humor… laughter does work.

Dedicated to Al-Anon groups everywhere.

30. Just Go Away

My husband would never bring me the one gift I always wanted from him: The gift of peace. I am a peaceful, loving, caring person. Yet many terrible, violent things have happened to me. I blamed God. I blamed myself. I blamed my parents. I blamed society. Did I ever blame the source? Did I ever put the blame where it belonged?

During my marriage, I prayed my husband would stop physically and mentally abusing me. I hoped he would change. I wished the little bit of good in him would overpower the bad. It didn't.

Yet after many punches, stitches, bruises, head-butts, abusive words—even after he raped me—I still felt sorry for him. I still cared about what happened to him. I wasn't sure if I loved him, but I did care. Most of all, I was afraid of him. I'll always be afraid of him. That's no lie.

As battered women, we need to stop wishing the violence will go away. Stop hoping he'll change. He won't change unless he gets professional help. Even then, he may not change. There is hope for an abuse-free tomorrow, but only if we are ready to change ourselves. Only if we are willing to stick to our decisions. It's a tough tunnel to walk through, but the light at the end is worth it!

Let us close today's reading with this: If there are many days throughout the year that your relationship brings you fear — get help! Give time, time. Don't make hasty decisions. In time, you will get your answers.

Dedicated to The Brown and Goldman Families.

31. The Years Go By

He started hitting me when I was only 16,
He was so vicious and so mean. Those fists of his felt like steel,
Followed by his "loving words" that were meant to heal.
"Sorry" was his favorite word,
After every beating, that's all I heard.
Broken promises and shattered dreams,
I thought a relationship was supposed to be a team.
More and more, I felt so trapped,
Through it all, I was able to adapt.
Adapt to living a life of hell,
Crying to myself, "Who could I tell?"
I told not a soul, as the years crept by,
So on and on, I gave it another try.
Trying and crying all the years through,
Begging and pleading, "That's not what husbands do!"
After many years of domestic abuse,
I decided to cut myself loose. Now here's where recovery must start,
No more violence, 'cause it's time for us to part!

Only you can stop the violence. Only you know when you've had enough abuse. Start your recovery today, because you may not have the chance tomorrow.

Dedicated to Janice, her boys and the violence they have endured.

32. RESPECT

How can you expect respect from others if you don't respect yourself? When your self-esteem is high, you feel better about who you are. You can love yourself if you respect who you are and what you believe in. Believing in yourself is difficult when you are constantly battered and degraded. Loving who you are inside and outside isn't easy when you have mental and physical scars.

Tell yourself in the mirror once (or more) a day, "I am a good person and I am worthy of respect." You begin to believe those words instead of the hurtful ones your abuser screams in your face. Replace the negative with the positive. You need to give yourself constructive characteristics, and soon you will believe them. Today, hold your head high, walk proud and smile long.

Dedicated to the Wednesday night support group. I love you all!

33. SELF-CARE

Are we selfish women for wanting a better a life for ourselves and for our children? NO! Every woman deserves a better life, free of abuse. I am not selfish because I love myself. I am not selfish because I take care of myself. I am not selfish because I no longer accept unacceptable behavior. By no means am I selfish for standing up for myself. I call it "self-care." Some people may think I am selfish because I fight for what I believe in. Outsiders tend to judge me based on what my ex-husband tells them. He makes me out to be someone I am not. Someone he made up so he doesn't have to look at what he's done. He pretends he is a good guy.

I hear gossip and lies about our relationship. I listen to mutual acquaintances inform me something I supposedly did or something he didn't do. Frustrating, yes but I try not to let it bother me to the point where I cannot function. My ex-husband knows the real truth and he has to live with his conscience...if he has one!

You are strong. You are courageous. You have the power to change if you are ready. Do give time time, but remember that this is your only life. Live it without domestic violence and live it without asking why!

Dedicated to Louise, a woman who has encountered many violent days.

35. Givers Verse Takers

Many times a battered women gets discouraged and frustrated because she feels she is the only one who gives in her life. She gives to her batterer. She gives to her children. She gives to her family. She gives to her employer. She keeps giving and giving. And while she is giving, she encounters many obstacles that discourage her even more.

There are "givers" and there are "takers" in the world we live in. Let us not waste any more time trying to figure out the "takers." Let us stop focusing on how much the "takers" have taken, and how little they have given. Let us continue giving, but let us never be doormats.

No matter how discouraged or frustrated the "takers" make us, let us remember this passage and never stop giving or striving for our light.

Dedicated to Manny and the abuse he has suffered.

36. Thinking Things Through

Do I like it when he beats me? Do I like it when he's kicking, slapping, punching, spitting, biting or throwing things at me? NO! Is it my fault that he does this to me? NO! I never asked to be hit. I never once said, "Hit me, beat me, kill me!" How dare others think that maybe I did deserve to be hurt by my husband.

I don't like these memories that cause me so much pain. The memories are sometimes as bad as the actual abuse was. Tears sting my eyes. The disgusting and demeaning words he spat at me hurt me again as I recall them.

I must face reality and decide if I want to continue this type of life and whether I wish to be beaten and abused for the rest of my days on earth. For my own safety, I must decide to leave or to stay. I know what the answer is; it's the footwork that scares me. It's not knowing that frightens me. The uncertainty of what will happen when I leave makes me have anxiety attacks. "At least when he's in my face, I know what to expect," I think to myself.

By accepting the truth for what it is, I can start making choices in my life. My life, not his life. I come first. I am the #1 person in my life. Sometimes reminding myself of that is enough to put things into perspective!

Dedicated to all companies that take the time to educate their employees on domestic violence.

37. ACCEPTANCE

Accept me for who I am. Accept me for my beliefs and my decisions. I pass no judgement on you. I can relate to other women in domestic violence situations. I can offer advice to the women who ask for my guidance, but at no time will I pass judgement on any woman for staying with or for leaving her abuser. I can only pray for her. I know I can only change myself. I can't change others who do not wish to be changed.

I've only walked in my own shoes, but I can relate to others. I can sympathize, empathize, disagree, and voice my opinion, but let me try not to judge others for their choices. Let me not push my opinion on others, especially if they don't ask for it.

Today, let me accept others for who they are and pray others will learn to accept me. There is a reason for everything on this planet. Let me not waste the precious time God gave me trying to figure them all out.

Dedicated to the women beaten by their partners today. May they find the strength and hope to seek help.

38. SUICIDE

I have thought about suicide time and again, but I never told anyone. To outsiders, I seem to be a strong woman. A woman who is doing it all. I'm raising three young boys as a single parent with a full-time career. People ask me all the time, "How do you do it?" "I just do. I don't think about it too much," I respond.

What they don't know is how I actually feel on the inside. How hard it truly is to be a single parent. To be the mother and the father. To get out of bed every day, knowing that three other human beings depend on me. That if I do not get up and act responsible, I could lose my job and my children. I am put in this position because the man I fell in love with, married, cared for and thought would be there to help me abused me emotionally, physically, sexually and financially.

When things get tough, I think sometimes about giving up. I wonder why my Higher Power chose me to struggle so much. My Higher Power has put many obstacles in my life, and I overcame them. I overcame domestic violence, so I know I can conquer anything I set my mind to. I strongly believe this. But, when my chips are down and the going gets tough, and depression, anxiety and tears set in, it is sometimes difficult to want to go on.

Let me take a moment to gather my thoughts. Let me breathe nice and slow. Let me hug my children, so I remember they need me as much as I need them. And, let me never forget ¼ of all suicide attempts are by battered women. Most of all, if those thoughts of suicide return, let me seek help right away to overcome them.

Dedicated to all women who have taken their lives due to domestic violence.

39. Do They Know?

Do others know what I feel? Do they know how deeply I hurt? Do they know how much I've changed because of domestic violence? Not if I choose not to tell them. Not if I keep my emotions bottled up inside.

Each time I was beaten, I changed. After he ridiculed me, tormented my soul and took advantage of my kindness, I lost a little part of who I was. I can accept the fact that over time, people change. Over time, we grow and learn. And when we go through life's experiences, we should become wiser. But when we are beaten down repeatedly and intimidated regularly, we change in another, sometimes, an unexplainable way.

When we could be trusting others, we turn away from them. When we could be giving love to our loved ones, we find it difficult to express our feelings. When we could be living free from violence, we shudder at the thought of our abuser coming home—a home to where the heart is not.

Let me begin this day by giving a hug, even if to only myself. Let me try to express my feelings more clearly to those I care about. Let me stop saying the words: could, should, and would, and start doing what is best for me. For when I start changing for the better, those who do not know how I feel, may be in for an eye-opener!

Dedicated to The Body Shop, for caring enough to campaign for women.

40. Choosing to Stay

Today I decided to give him one more chance. He doesn't know I was even thinking about leaving him. No one knows, but it's on my mind 24 hours a day. Even when I sleep, thoughts about leaving him consume my dreams.

This morning I decided it would be best to stay in this abusive relationship. I am in fear of my life all the time, but at least I know what to expect. If I tell the police to make him leave, or if I leave, who knows what will happen. I am worried that he may hurt himself, me, or God only knows who else.

Guilt overwhelms me when I consider leaving him. He loves me...doesn't he? He doesn't mean to hit me. He doesn't mean those terrible names he calls me. He said he wouldn't hit me again. But he said that before! All these thoughts race through my confused mind. I need to slow down my thinking. I have to rest for a while and try not to worry about it today. I am not ready to make a decision now.

Not making a decision is making a decision, though. I need to think. I know I am exactly where I need to be for now. I will work with my Higher Power to make any life-altering decisions. Just for today, I will stay. Tomorrow a different decision may be waiting for me. When I am ready to leave, I will know it. When I have had enough abuse, I will know that, too.

Dedicated to Elaine, my sister, my friend.

41. 4:00 A.M.

It's that time again, beating time. Sunday morning, when the cocaine has run out and the beer is all gone, he stumbles home.

"Wake up you bitch—move over!" He doesn't have to tell me to wake up, because I'm not sleeping. The anxiety and fear that had been lurking since before he came home escalate when he arrives. He's ready to fight and I don't want to, but that doesn't matter. He cusses at me, then kicks me in the back. I fall off the bed. He lies next to me and starts saying disgusting words in my ear. He wants to have sex with me, but I refuse. This only makes him madder. He grabs my hair and drags me across the floor. I cry and plead with him to stop. He lifts me up by my hair and without notice, head butts me, knocking me down again. He leaves me on the floor and goes to sleep on the couch.

Sound familiar? If so, then it's time for you to get help. Reach out to the many organizations for women located in the back of this book, telephone hotlines, family members, friends or whomever you can trust. There are people and places that will help you if you are ready and willing to leave the world of domestic violence. Sure, you will have difficult times over the next few days, weeks, months and years, but it is better to struggle without suffering abuse.

I leave you with this: pull my hair no more, never head butt me again; punch me in the face only in your dreams. I am ready to change. I am ready to stop the violence that could eventually kill me — and I don't want to die! Not today, not tomorrow, and certainly not on someone else's terms.

Dedicated to Pam S. for sharing what she's gone through.

42. Survival/Why Stay?

Survival is the key today. We stayed because we needed to remain alive. His threats were too real to ignore. His fists were always present. His words too harsh not to listen to. His eyes too devilish not to turn away. It's not easy for a battered woman to walk out the door.

It takes time, courage, strength, a Higher Power, self-esteem and the truth to finally end the relationship. Many times we attempt to leave, but we are not ready so we go back. But when we're finally ready, we struggle every day for months, or even years, before the effects of that abusive relationship begin to fade. We struggle with guilt, fear and anxiety — emotions so powerful, we think our heads will explode. "Why stay?" people ask.

Survival. We stayed to survive. We survived for many years in our abusive relationship. Some take an entire decade to accept their abuser for who he is and understand he is not willing to change his unhealthy behavior.

Today, allow me to see the word "survival" in a new light. You stayed for your reasons, and I stayed for mine, but in the end, we stayed to survive. Let us pray for all women surviving today.

Dedicated to Dr. Marleen Harmon in New Jersey. Her honesty and openness has touch many battered women.

43. EMERGENCY

What do I do in an emergency? If I am prepared, all I need to do is take one or two steps and I can be in a safe place sooner. We prepare for a fire by installing smoke alarms in our homes. We have locks on our doors and windows to keep intruders out. We may have a car alarm so our cars will not be stolen. We may even carry mace with us, so we feel safe from assault. But what do we do to stay safe when we're being victimized in our homes?

When a violent situation occurs, things don't usually go smoothly. Do your best to have a "plan A" and a "plan B." And whatever you do, get to a safe place as quickly as you can! These tips can help you in a dangerous situation:

- Go to a friend's or family member's house (someone you can trust).

- Go to a local shelter, one that's further away from your home, if putting distance between you and your abuser helps you feel safe.

- Put aside money for a hotel. It doesn't have to be a lot, just enough for you (and your children) to stay a night or two until you think things through.

- Keep an extra car key hidden so you can make a quick getaway.
- Have emergency numbers near the phone. You may need to call the police. (You may even want to set up a "ring system" with a friend or family member. Ring twice and then hang up. This means you need someone to call you right back or call the police for you.)
- Keep change accessible so you can make a call from a pay phone.
- Keep a small overnight bag packed with a few essential hidden somewhere. If you know whose home you will stay at, hide your bag there.

This is your life. Do not take for granted that you will be in a calm state of mind to remember what you need. Plan now for an emergency tomorrow. Hopefully that emergency will never happen, but it's better to be safe than sorry.

Dedicated to emergency rooms treating victims of domestic violence with care and compassion.

44. His Begging

"Please forgive me. Don't leave me. You don't really want to press charges. You don't really want to lock me up. I love you. I didn't mean to hurt you. I didn't mean to say those things. You know I don't mean what I say. I told you I can change. Let me stay the night. Let me hold you. I need you. I can't live without you. I will kill myself if you leave me."

Sound too familiar? He is an expert at begging. He begs until he gets me to give in to his lies. I give in to his desperate pleadings. I give in to his tears of forgiveness, tears that I've fallen for so many times before. "If only he would not beg me," I think to myself. If he wouldn't cry, maybe I could leave him. My "if onlys" go on and on. My denial mechanism kicks in. It's my way of not having to change. It's my way of not dealing with the abuse.

Instead of feeling for me, I feel for him. I turn off my feelings altogether so I can take care of his needs. I am convinced that his feelings are more important than mine. He makes me believe he can't live without me. I need to focus on what his begging and pleading is doing to me.

If I can focus on the reason(s) he is begging me for forgiveness, then I may be able to begin seeing him for who he is. I might begin to see what he has done that makes him beg. This day that I chose to survive, let me allow more acceptance into my life.

Let me take time to read this page again to think things through.

Dedicated to those who have written books on domestic violence.

45. Loving an Abusive Partner

Love. I am lost for words. Love. I love a person who hurts me almost every day. Love. This four-letter word should mean peaceful things; instead it brings thoughts that make me shake my head in wonder. Love. I wanted to love him so much that he would have to stop hurting me. Love. I tried to love him more, so things wouldn't be that bad. Love. I convinced myself that I would never love another. Love. I believed I had no choice but to pretend to love him. Love...

I need to be okay with the simple fact that I love a person who abuses me. My love for him may be simple, but what he is doing to me is not. Whatever my decisions are about our relationship, I need to understand in my heart that it is not my fault that I love him. It is not my fault that I care for him. Only in time can I begin to change how I feel about this person who does me wrong. In time, I may learn I can still love him and live without him. Time, it may not heal all wounds, but it is what I need to change.

Dedicated to Tia, who died violently at the hands of her boyfriend at age 21.

46. Who Understands Me? Only a Few...

Walk in my shoes for only a day,
Run in my shoes because there's hell to pay.
You'll pay with a put-down, punch, or a kick,
The feelings of loneliness will make you so sick.
Miles and miles you'll walk in my shoes,
Miles of pain, suffering, and feeling the blues.
Walking and crying and feeling like dying,
Will you walk in my shoes and keep on trying?

Many people who have never been abused by a loved one do not relate to those who have. They say we are fools to stay with our abusers. They judge us without knowing who we really are and what we stand for. All of you who are or were abused, find a therapist who deals with domestic violence or women who have formed support groups. There are some free programs for women and some offer payment plans. Call your local women's group. Please look in the back of this book for a local or toll-free number. There is hope. There is help if you are ready for it.

Remember, only those who have walked in your shoes truly understand about what you are feeling. Share your pain and feelings with those who do not judge you. Share with those who can understand you. You are not alone!

Dedicated to Sherry who was murdered by her husband. (Let us take a moment to pray for those domestic violence victims that were murdered by their partners.)

47. VERBAL ABUSE

Don't think he's not abusing you when he is not hitting you. If you think he's not mentally abusing you because he never hit you or only hit you once or twice—you're wrong! Abuse is abuse. A wonderful woman I met thought her boyfriend didn't abuse her because he never hit her or verbally abused her. Well, he mentally abused her by staying away for days at a time. He called her when he was high on cocaine and begged her forgiveness. He would always call her to get him out of unpleasant situations. He would call her at all hours of the night to come get him. He would call her and cry to her because he loved her and he hated himself for doing drugs and drinking alcohol. Does this sound all too familiar to you? If it does, you are being abused mentally. No one deserves to be abused. No woman should go through any type of abuse.

Mental abuse means control. It lowers your self-esteem. It reduces your confidence. When you hear negative comments over and over again from the same person you eventually start believing they're true. When that happens, try to turn negative into positive. Don't jeopardize your situation, but don't be a doormat either.

Remember what a wonderful woman you are and think of the good qualities you have to offer any man, woman or child. Don't settle for any less than you can give!

Dedicated to my brother, Michael T., for stopping by to talk and calling me from Europe.

48. Fears and Frustrations

I will be looking over my shoulder my entire life, waiting to see my ex-husband watching me. His behavior has affected the way I feel about my surroundings. I am almost always afraid. It's frustrating!

Since my abuser left my house, I haven't gone outside without glancing around for him. My head rests on my pillow each night remembering the pain he caused me and my family. Somehow, some way, his face or name comes to my mind. It's frustrating!

I wonder how I make it through some days without breaking down. I keep busy and pray that he doesn't do anything bad to me. When I wake up every morning, my Higher Power gets a thanks for allowing me to "rise and shine."

When I start projecting about my abuser, my thoughts need to be refocused. I need to tell myself my circumstances will get better. I need to remember to always keep my hope alive. Some days, it's all I have.

Dedicated to Frank for his patience, kindness, honesty, friendship and unconditional love. Thanks for allowing me to check and recheck all the doors.

49. A Day to Think About My Accomplishments

Today let me think about how far I've come, not how far I have to go. If I take this day to acknowledge my successes and accomplishments, then my attitude can only be gratitude. Even if I woke up this morning feeling depressed or sad, let me try and end those negative feelings with a "success list" today.

Success is anything from waking up on a gloomy day to graduating high school to getting a minimum wage job to passing the bar exam to ending an abusive relationship to surviving another day. My successes are what I make them. Give me the strength to pat myself on the back for the little accomplishments as well as the big ones. I should be proud of all that I do, today and every day of my life.

Success List of the Day:

—

—

—

—

Dedicated to Marilyn's friendship and for sharing her family with me.

50. THE SAME OLD THING

When do you have to be sick and tired of being sick and tired? Everyone has a different tolerance. Working with my support groups, I've met a lot of women at different stages in their lives. Some have had enough, and some hadn't. Some were ready to change, some were just beginning and some said, "No way, change." A few have said, "He's the one that's gotta change!" After a while, I came to my own conclusion: I was the only one that could change my situation. He certainly didn't want to change and he was the one causing most of our problems.

My opinion is we all have our own limits. Boundaries are different for each person. I can't remember what went on in my mind the day I had my husband removed from our home. Something just "clicked" inside me and there was no going back. Something productive needed to be done about my situation or my children would start to pay for his actions. They were only 6, 3 and 1 then. Children adjust to their surroundings. For me, allowing them to adjust to their father abusing their mother was unacceptable.

Be patient with yourself if you are going through similar problems at this point in your life. Listen to your feelings. Share your feelings with people you can trust. You need to know help and support are out there. You also have to realize, unfortunately, that you are the one who has to do most of the footwork. In time, you will learn that the footwork is well worth the light at the end of your tunnel.

Dedicated to my two grandmothers. I love them and I will always cherish them.

51. ANGER

ANGER at my abuser for...
    hitting me.
    kicking me.
    biting me.
    pulling my hair.
    dragging me across the floor.
    spitting in my face.
    calling me degrading names.
    sending me to the hospital.
    raping me.
    giving me stitches.
    not financially supporting his children.
    staying out all night.
    showing me no respect.
    choosing alcohol and drugs over his family.
    gambling...and losing.
    his dagger-eye looks.
    stealing from me.
    mentally abusing me.
    telling his children he'll be there...and not showing up.
    stalking me.
    sentencing me to a life that is full of unnecessary fears.

Today give me the extra courage to let go of one of these angry items on my list. Letting go can help reduce my angry feelings. Letting go of the past lifts the heavy weight off my shoulders.

Dedicated to Sue and Bill for opening your home to Blaine and I during the worst week of our lives.

52. Letting Go

Letting go of the past is difficult to do. It is a daily struggle. Knowing I have no control over what happened to me in the past is frustrating. But my focus should be on controlling what happens to me today. Living in the past is not healthy for me. It gets me down and will keep me down if I let it. I cannot erase the abuse that I've suffered, but I can change the way I live today and the way I will live tomorrow.

Learning to let go of my frustration and helplessness at not being able to control another person's actions is my focus on this day. That means when my partner lashes out at me with hurtful words after he's had a tough day at work, let me remind myself it is not my fault. It's his fault if he hits me, kicks me, punches me or pulls my hair. It means if he chooses to take drugs or abuse alcohol, I cannot prevent it, or be responsible for what he does. I am not accountable for my partner's actions.

Letting go means letting go of so very much. It means letting go of the daily guilt, the projection, the fears and the uncertainty of change. Best of all, the beauty in letting go means becoming healthier.

Dedicated to Liz Claiborne for their dedication to women's issues.

53. Fears

Afraid...
> to look at him.
> to speak to him.
> to speak up for myself.
> to be late, he's a jealous one.
> when he drinks or uses drugs.
> when my next beating will come.
> when he'll degrade me again.
> he'll kill me.
> he'll rape me again.
> of hand movements too close to my face.
> having my doors unlocked.
> to fall in love with someone else.
> he'll hurt someone I care about.

Perpetual fear is something I've acquired over the years from my abusive relationship. I will always be afraid of my abuser, no matter what. Even if he dies, I fear his ghost will haunt me. It may sound odd, but it's not when you're a woman in an abusive relationship.

Let me try to work on my fear or let me write my fears down so I can work on them one at a time. After I see a difference, allow me the courage to move on and vanquish the next fear.

Dedicated to Marie and her pain caused by family violence.

54. Flashbacks

Lately, flashbacks happen when I see an unlocked door, hear his name, see a person being hit on television, talking about abuse, or touch the parts of my body where scars from my abuser remain.

As I sit on a park bench watching my children play, the warm sun shines on my face—I smile. Suddenly, I want to cry. Why? Is it because I heard someone say something or saw someone that brought back a painful memory? Could it be I rubbed my eyes and felt the tiny bumps in my eye socket from being hit? (Always in the face.) Or, could it be the fact that I'm raising my three children by myself? No, it's not the children. I'm so proud to be capable of raising my three boys on my own. Having them grow up in a home where there's no violence, a home that has one healthy parent instead of two unhealthy ones, gives me peace.

I'm smiling again because I'm alive and my boys are happy and healthy. So I get off the bench, pick up my youngest son, put him in the swing and enjoy the moment. The pain of being abused and the pain of dealing with it must wait for now. In a way, my son's smile as he swings is therapy enough. When another flashback comes, let me try my best to deal with it. Maybe I'll be fortunate that a happy moment will overpower my flashback. If that doesn't happen, I'll remember my tunnel and walk toward the light. I will walk at my own pace.

Be thankful for today. Be thankful you are alive. And be thankful there is hope.

Dedicated to Susan C. for sharing her own family abuse story.

55. YES, IT WAS REALLY THAT BAD!

She is curled up on the floor hoping he will just vanish. She's bleeding, angry, fearful and she's alone sobbing until he leaves the room. She stares at the wall and sees nothing but despair. Breathing heavily, she calms herself only to hear him laughing at her. He makes rude comments loud enough for her to hear. She does not move until she is sure he's sleeping. She uses the bed to steady herself and she stands. Dizzy from him pulling clumps of hair out of her head, she sits on the edge of the bed. Her legs shake as she stands to look at herself in the mirror. She has been through this before. She only wants to cover her bruises from others. She doesn't think of herself. She thinks only about what everyone will say when they see her. Dreaming up excuses for this time so they will be different from last time. She wants to tell him she's sorry he beat her. She wants to say she's sorry for standing up to him. She wants to tell him everything is okay and she believes he loves her. She knows his words already. She knows that he will beg her forgiveness and tell her he did not mean to hit her. He'll tell her he loves her. She questions herself if he really loves her. As she washes the blood away, she washes the experience away too. Maybe she will not have to go out. Maybe she will not see anyone she knows. Maybe she can cover the marks long enough for them to fade. Maybe no one will ever know…

…but she knows.

This woman's name is your name. You may be this woman, even if you have not been physically abused, even if your story differs slightly. All women affected by domestic violence have similar memories which will last a lifetime. Any kind of abuse hurts. If you think you can cover up your domestic violence problems, think again. Stop washing away your painful memories and start learning from them today.

Dedicated to Lavern P. for her willingness to share her domestic violence stories.

56. Living in the Present, Not the Past

Remember way back when...

    ...you were in grammar school?

    ...you thought you'd never kiss a boy?

    ...you got your period?

    ...you went on your first date?

    ...you called your parents, mommy and daddy?

    ...you fell in love?

Remember when...

    ...you met your abuser?

    ...he hit you?

    ...you had your first black eye?

    ...you made your first excuse for the bruises?

    ...you waited all night for him to come home?

    ...he abused you when he finally came home?

    ...you apologized for being abused?

    ...he called you horrible names?

    ...you thought he'd never stop hurting you?

    ...you thought he was going to kill you?

Remember this...

...you are a good person and don't deserve to be abused.

...you don't have to accept unacceptable behavior.

...you can get support and stop the violence.

...you can live an abuse-free life.

...you can have a life of happiness.

...you can like who you are and be proud of yourself.

...you don't need a person who treats you without respect.

...you can walk through your tunnel and touch the light.

...if you have children, make a better life for them...for yourself...and free yourself from domestic violence.

Take one day at a time and be proud of who you are.

Dedicated to Rhonda for sharing her most intimate life stories.

57. WRITTEN ASSIGNMENT

Today is a day for you to write down your thoughts. Take this page and write what you like about yourself. If you cannot write, then think. Or you may want to start a journal today. My thoughts and prayers are with you.

Dedicated to the author of this page.

58. EMPOWERMENT

Empowerment is the word for the day. Being able to empower yourself today — even for five minutes — will help build self-esteem.

If you embrace the opportunity to empower yourself then you will gain strength. And sometimes the best strength comes from within.

Why not take the time to empower yourself with knowledge today. Learn something you might not have known or didn't want to admit before about victims of domestic violence. Take the next few minutes to read the following statistics. Empower yourself.

— Battering frequently increases during pregnancy.

— Each year more than one million Americans are stalked.

— 1/4 of all suicide attempts are made by battered women; and this rises to 1/2 for African American women.

— National Domestic Violence Hotline 1-800-799-SAFE.

Dedicated to Kit for her dedication to the women in New York.

59. Success and What it Means

We all view success differently. Some believe success is graduating from high school. To some it's a first home. To others it may be a new baby or moving up the corporate ladder. These are ordinary goals many people take for granted. But those who have been affected by family violence may see success in an entirely different light.

To those who have struggled and are struggling with abuse of any kind, success may mean eating one meal a day. Success to a homeless person may be sleeping indoors on a rainy night. And success to a victim of domestic violence may be not being abused in an hour or not getting stitches this month. Success to a child who sees his or her mother being tortured may be sleeping at grandma's house tonight. Or, sadly enough, success may be surviving another day with his gun pointed at your head.

Success is what we make it. Success is how we feel on the inside and how we look at ourselves on the outside. As long as I make it through this day, let me accept it for the immense success it is.

Dedicated to Mom and Augie and our dinner talks.

60. Violence and Culture

Sometimes domestic violence perpetrators defend themselves by claiming that what they are doing is part of their culture.

Violence is NOT part of culture. Culture is different from traditions of violence and domination. Culture is the collection of shared practices, often including language, foods, rituals of celebration and religious or spiritual beliefs. Culture unites, enriches and creates an experience of belonging and promotes a common history among all members of a group of people.

Take today to think whether or not your culture has yet to set up boundaries separating violence from the rest of your shared practices.

Dedicated to Ken and Rhea for their unselfish efforts to educate people on diversity.

61. He May Never See His Light

Just like some women never see their light at the beginning of their tunnel, your abuser may never see his light. All those involved in family violence have various tolerance levels. They have their own amounts of patience. They have boundaries to set. We may want to believe that every woman affected by domestic violence will find her own way out of her relationship. We also have hope our abuser will stop hurting us, that he will change his unacceptable behavior and magically change back into the man we fell in love with.

What we need to accept is that even when our abuser sees the stars in the sky, he may never see the light. Even when we realize that domestic violence is no longer in our cards, our abuser may not change his deck. Even when we make those phone calls to get him help, drive him to a rehab or a place for men that batter, we cannot do his footwork for him. We have all tried to make him stop abusing us. We have begged him. We have pleaded with him. We have loved him as much as we possibly can. All these things have not helped his behavior so far, so what makes us continue to think they will eventually change him?

I cannot change my abuser. He is responsible for changing himself, just as I am responsible for changing me.

Let me remember today that I cannot make a blind man see, nor a deaf man hear, so what makes me think I can make an abusive man stop abusing? Accepting others for who they are will help me in my own recovery.

Dedicated to my brother Allan and his fiancé Donna for their love and friendship.

62. Cuts Like a Knife

Hits and kicks may break my bones,
But words would always hurt me.
Yell and scream and put me down,
For mental scars you can't see!
Mental scars go deep within,
A woman's head and heart.
Cuts like a knife the words he roars,
Like bitch and slut and whore!
In time your head can't tell apart,
The words for love and hate.
But give time time I'll tell you this,
Abuse is not your fate!

Re-read today's poem and decide for yourself how your life is affected by another's verbal abuse.

Dedicated to John and Katie for their suffering.

63. Is His Love Enough?

Is the love our abusers give us enough to last our entire lives? Are we content to stay in an unbalanced relationship that causes us pain, suffering and humiliation? Each of you that reads today's passage will have to ask yourself these questions. We all have different tunnels to walk through, but every one leads to the same fork in the road. A road on which, in time, we will stop and ask for directions. We'll stop and see if we are taking the correct path. We'll stop and think about which road to keep walking in our lives.

As human beings, we crave love. We crave happiness. We crave peace and serenity. We need to feel loved and feel others caring, as well as sharing their happiness with us. Being in an abusive relationship only makes us crave these things even more. Love, happiness, peace and serenity are missing from our relationship with our abuser. Instead, we feel anger, hatred, depression, loneliness, fear, shame and many more negative feelings. So is the question, "is his love enough," answered today? For me, it is. His love is not enough. It never was and never will be enough for me. But remember, that is my answer. Each of us has different answers because we are all in different places today. We all have to work through our feelings one at a time. Some of us may be ready to accept we will never be loved enough by our abusers, and others of us may believe we are satisfied with the level of love we receive. Whatever you feel is okay. It is where you are today and no one can take that from you. Have patience with yourself to work through any feelings you may be experiencing today or will experience tomorrow.

Love for others is in each of our minds and hearts. Let us show love to ourselves as well.

Dedicated to my three beautiful sons, Blaine, Derek and Travis.

64. PERSONAL WARS

Our government sends troops to foreign countries to "keep the peace." On my worst days living with my abuser, I wish for those troops to rescue me. Daily, I do my best to "keep the peace," between myself and my husband. I try to keep my mouth shut when he is verbally abusing me. By not giving in to his verbal harassment, I win a small battle in my war against domestic violence.

Domestic violence can be like a fight on a battle field. There are land mines and unexpected traps set by my husband — the enemy. He sits and waits while I fall victim to his traps, lies and manipulation. Living in his prison I become weaker as the years go by. My self-esteem decreases. My eyes shed tears. My life turns into a whirlwind, full of harmful things blocking my view to recovery. I grow more desperate each day, but not until I hit bottom do I look for an escape route from his prison.

I do not give up hope when my prison cell closes each night. By keeping my hopes and dreams alive, I do not go through with thoughts of suicide, thoughts of killing the enemy or other desperate alternatives. Instead, by looking through the cracks in my cell, I see that help is out there. I seek that help and thrive upon its understanding and warmth. After years of falling victim to the enemy's traps, I walk over them with caution and pride.

I am no longer a victim. I am a survivor of war. My personal war with domestic violence is now on my terms. I've made a peace agreement with myself because I am the only one that counts, and the only one who can make such an agreement.

Dedicated to Betty C., who I never knew, yet I feel connected to.

65. Should I Stay or Should I Go?

Sometimes I wonder why I stay in this abusive relationship. Why do I stay and put up with all the pain and suffering? Do I really know what the answer is? Yes, I think I do. The reality is, I am afraid of change. I am afraid of what may or may not happen to me. I am fearful of the unknown. I know that if I stay with my abuser, he will continue to abuse me. I also know that if I leave, I will be without him for the first time. Wow, that's scary!

It's time to consider my options. I need to write down my thoughts to clear my head. There are so many choices to make, so many questions to ask myself. I may also have things to say to my abuser. And I'm not just worried about myself. What about my children? What will I tell them?

If I really want to get out of my abusive relationship, then let me think things through and make sure I have at least two plans. This way, if something goes wrong with my first plan, I have a back-up. God, give me courage and strength to follow through with my decisions. Grant me the tools to stay focused. Help me not to question my decision to leave. My choices are my own choices, and I need to accept them.

Remember, you can only make decisions based on what you know. Allow yourself time to seek help and find support. You will learn moré than you can imagine through sharing and through listening to others in similar relationships.

Dedicated to battered women's shelters everywhere and the many volunteers that give the gift of their time.

66. Regrets

I was beaten and raped by my husband in 1988. I never pressed charges. Do I regret it? Honestly, I don't know. I try to live without regrets because they only keep me down. My life is too short for regrets. I must live today knowing that I made the best choices I could at that difficult time in my life.

I was so young when I was raped. I was a different person then. I allowed others to make a lot of decisions for me concerning the rape and the beatings. I can't change the past. I have to let it go. I must try not to dwell on it. What I want to do now is share my experiences with women who have been through the same terrors I have. Sharing my past and listening to women who are currently in abusive relationships enables me to release some of my own pain. By sharing my story I can also give others hope that no matter what their past decisions, they can overcome them.

If you were raped or sexually abused by your partner, talk about it. Call a hotline, see a therapist, go to a support group or talk to someone you can trust. Your pain won't melt away, but sharing it will help.

Just for today, my regrets will cease. Let me acknowledge a past mistake or difficult time in my life, but let me close this book accepting that difficult time for what it was, not for what it could have been.

Dedicated to Carla in Chicago, an inspiration to battered women everywhere.

67. Details of Rape

I can remember him raping me like it was yesterday. My stomach turns at the thought. He gave me my worst beating that night too. How I cried, screamed out in anger, in fear, in pain, in need of someone's help. If only someone heard my screams. I was so humiliated! The police officers were so cold to me! The hospital bathroom was so disgusting. I also remember how the doctor looked at me as he took my pubic hair samples and how the nurse hurt me as she took blood from my left arm.

These details may not sound important, but they will resound for a lifetime in my head. A lifetime. I was talked out of pressing charges by the detectives, especially the female officer. She told me that rape is hard to prove between a husband and a wife, even with all of my bruises and cuts, the blood, and the samples they took at the hospital. Why then, did they make me go through those disgusting and embarrassing tests? I could have been home sleeping. I could have been lying in the dark with myself instead of with strangers who cared less what happened to me, and even less about the violence against me. They would have done me more justice if they told me to go home and get some sleep, instead of taking pictures of my face and body. Instead of making me answer questions.

If I sound bitter it's because I am still suffering. All women who have been sexually abused have the right to feel betrayed. To feel pain. To feel cast aside by others who look at them with, "that look." But for today, I must learn to live with the fact that I did not press charges. On this day, let me begin to forgive myself for something I had no control over. Let me release my bitterness.

Dedicated to Elizabeth and her five sons.

68. Recognizing Abuse

Every room in the house. His mother's house. His brother's backyard. In front of our children. In other towns. On the floor next to our bed. A wedding. The Superbowl. In the car. A friend's house. When he was high. When he was sober. Lights on. Lights off. When I was sixteen. When I was twenty-six. 3:00 p.m. 3:00 a.m. New Year's Eve. Our son's christening.

Abuse happens in many different places. It happens lots of times and in a number of ways. It's not important where or when it happens; it's sill abuse! Recognizing that you are being abused is a major step in your tunnel of violence. It doesn't matter whether you are mentally abused, verbally abused or physically abused—abuse is abuse!

For the first few years with my abuser, I didn't think about the abuse. I accepted it as part of my life, our life together. I believed I had no other choice but to accept the violence. I thought I deserved to be battered and verbally abused. After thinking a great deal about my situation, I finally realized that being hurt by my husband was not normal. It was time for me to get some help.

Today, stop and think about your life of abuse. Consider some of the places or events at which you have been abused. By thinking of exact situations, you may be able to see a ray of light and make that phone call to stop the violence. You have the power and the right to change.

Dedicated to Stu for getting involved in my personal crisis. Without his kind and encouraging words, I might not be here today.

69. Outside Looking In

Those who are not affected by family violence ridicule women who tolerate their partners' abuse. Outsiders cannot fathom how much women and children suffer at the fists and harsh words of a batterer. Being a battered woman is like being a prisoner of war. Only it's a war of the heart that leaves battle scars long after the fight is over.

Domestic violence is not the fault of women who choose to stay and make the best of their abusive situations. The women who stay are not ready to leave yet, or do not know how to escape from their prisons. Some women chisel away year after year, trying to break free. When they reach various levels of breaking away, they get scared and try to plaster the pieces back together. Some battered women do this time and again. It sometimes takes a lifetime of digging an underground tunnel to get to a safe haven and the freedom it can bring.

Wherever you may be in your tunnel of violence, do not blame yourself for being there. You are doing your best. Keep digging. Keep searching. Your freedom from domestic violence can come to you if you are ready and willing to take the steps to break free.

Dedicated to The Women's Crisis Service of Hunterdon County, New Jersey.

70. FUTURE PENALTIES

Will society penalize me after I've escaped domestic violence? Haven't I suffered enough without others placing more blame on me, the victim and survivor?

After reading about a woman who gave love, not only to her own children but to a foster child, I wrote this page. With mandatory parenting classes and the state's consent behind her, she began to care for this foster child. Over a year later, she was denied the right to continue caring for and loving the child based on her past relationship with her estranged husband. Records showed that she had called the police a few times during their marriage because he verbally abused her so the state agency took the foster baby from her. She informed the agency that she had been separated more than three years since her training to be a foster parent, and that she was an upstanding member of her community. Unfortunately, her state's foster care agency punished her for getting out of her abusive relationship.

Domestic violence with all its deadly dominoes affects not only women and children who suffer from it, but also those who struggled to escape its clutches. And after reading this page, you may realize that domestic violence affects even those who have not been directly touched by it. I am referring to the foster child who finally had a mother to show him love and warmth, until he was wrongfully taken from her arms because she chose not to remain a victim.

Today, no matter how others may seem to judge me, let me try my best to do what's right for me.

Dedicated to Kelly in Holmdel, New Jersey for walking toward her first doorway to freedom.

71. LEAVING

Statistics show that a battered woman is in the most danger when she attempts to leave her abuser or change her situation.

So, what can you do? You need to consider your options and make plans. You also need to accept that your plans might not go as smoothly as you hoped.

Leaving the man who has abused, controlled and dominated your life will most likely cause a fight. He may or may not believe you will leave him. He may let you go without a glance. You won't be able to see the future, but you can pray to your Higher Power to give you the strength to help you leave for good.

But whether you're leaving this time for good or not, tell yourself to be strong. Pray for that strength. Pray for courage. Just like the cowardly lion who had courage all along—you do too!

Dedicated to my dad who has been a strength to lean on and who has fought his own personal battle because of his daughter's abusive relationship.

72. Cowards

Men who beat their loved ones are not men, they are cowards. They are chickens, pantywaists, sissies and wimps. They are cowards who don't take responsibility. They are cowards who don't want to get help. They are cowards who don't want to change their patterns. Cowards like these who abuse their wives have no self-esteem. A coward is a wife-beater and a wife-beater is a coward.

Before my recovery program, I thought my ex-husband was brave. I believed that he had strength, courage and power. His ability to control me was amazing. He made me believe he would always control me and that I couldn't leave. He manipulated me into thinking I had to stay and take his abuse.

It wasn't until I started getting help for my low self-esteem, and the physical and mental abuse that I realized my husband was a coward.

Today, allow me enough courage to take a step in the direction of my own recovery.

Dedicated to Jean Auel and Alya. The emotions they have helped me face cannot be put into words.

73. CRYING

When I cry in bed at night, does anyone hear my tears? How can they hear when the pillow silences my sorrow, my pain, my fear? I hear my tears, though. To me, they sound like a deafening explosion.

I lay still, hoping he won't wake me. I'm praying that he'll just walk out our front door. I'm wishing the bruises he just gave me will not be there in the morning. But I know this isn't reality. Intellectually I understand he won't change. I know my tears of pain won't simply fade out of my life, but my emotions engulf my intellect and the crying begins again.

Just for today, let me lie in bed with serenity on my mind. If I need to cry, let it happen. After a few tears have fallen, let me relax and dream of the peaceful moments awaiting me. Give me the knowledge that crying is healing and healing is growing and growing is learning—so let me cry.

Dedicated to Mary from Milwaukee for connecting with me during the difficult times we shared as two battered women.

74. Sex

Does the word sex repulse me? It does when it's associated with my abuser. The smell of liquor on his breath is so disgusting, I cannot even kiss him. The cocaine matted to his nostrils sickens me. There's no love at all in his cold eyes. His reflexes are so pathetic, if he tries to lay down in bed he'll land on the floor. Words of anger, hatred, self-pity, insecurity and confusion fly from his lips, and he's making no sense at all.

This is how my abuser looked many times when he wanted to have sex with me. On a bad day, I appeased him and went through with it just so he would leave me alone. Sometimes ignoring him or giving him the cold shoulder would work. On a good day, he left me alone.

Whatever works for you, go with it. (I went with my gut.) Whatever you decide, it is your body. You are the one who has to live with your decisions. Do what is healthy for you. If you are in an uncomfortable situation, think things over.

Take a five-minute time out and make the best choice you can. Whatever the outcome, know that it's just for today, and that's a start.

Dedicated to Debra, who was bludgeoned to death by her boyfriend.

75. ABUSED MEN

Today is a day for us to think about the 5-8% of men who are battered by their female partners. Yes, some men are physically and mentally abused by their partners.

In talking to a few women who have been victims of domestic violence (or know a victim) I found out many know a man who is being battered.

Today is a day to pray for all victims of domestic violence—men included. Today is a day to look in a mirror and believe that we can change the cycle of violence and end the abuse we're all enduring. By praying or thinking about all victims of domestic violence, we may not feel so alone. And if some of those victims are men, give us the wisdom to accept them like we accept women who are battered. Give us the will to keep our minds open.

Dedicated to the thousands of men who are battered each year.

76. THE RIDE OF MY LIFE

How often do we ride the same roller coaster? One that causes us to throw up, gives us bodily injuries, depletes the money in our pockets, makes us wait two hours for a five-minute ride, and instills fear in us as we wait to become its victim all over again?

My life has become a never-ending roller coaster ride. Even as I comprehend the past, present and future, I continue to allow the roller coaster to get the best of me. I knowingly give in to its scare tactics and its wrongdoings as well as what happens to me when the ride ends. I really do not like roller coasters, but right now, they are all I know.

If my roller-coaster ride continues with its loops, turns, screams, physical strains, and the before and after mental affects, I may jump off the tracks while the ride is in progress, instead of waiting until the operator ends it. Or maybe I should wait until the ride slows. Maybe that tranquility is what I need most.

Give me the strength today to get off of my roller coaster. Let me keep my feet on the ground and not be a victim to the ups and downs in my life taking me for a ride.

Dedicated to K.C., a woman who sometimes rides a merry-go-round instead of a usual roller coaster.

77. But He Does Keep the House Clean...

...I said these exact words to my therapist! "He still has one good quality, he keeps the house clean." How ridiculous is that? Depending where you are in your recovery, making positive statements about your abuser may or may not be your "cup of tea."

Trying to hold on to the last good quality or positive thing my abuser did was my way of keeping him in my life physically and emotionally. After he beat me, he would make up for it by cleaning our apartment, scrubbing the kitchen floor, buying me something, or taking care of my wounds. This was his way to end the overpowering guilt he had for abusing me.

I should not blame myself for grasping at the last remaining straws he puts in front of me. I should not focus on his one or two good qualities because by doing so, I remain in this unhealthy situation longer than I need to. Holding onto his last positive quality begins the "maybe he can change "stage or the "he's not that bad" stage or the "he does love me" stage or the "maybe if I tried harder" stage. All these stages will continue in my life if I allow them to. If I do not accept the fact that he may never change, a month, a year, or 10 years from now, I may be in the same place I am today.

Abuse of any kind is a cycle that takes years to recover from. Abuse in any form is devastating. So the question here is not whether he has any good qualities, but whether his positive qualities outweigh his negative ones, and whether or not I can remain a part of his destructive life.

Dedicated to Judy for trying to understand her sister's choice to stay.

78. AGAINST THE WIND

As Bob Seger sings, "*I'm still running against the wind,*" I wipe the tear running down my cheek. I think about how many days I've walked into a wind caused by the breath of the person I married. I think about how many nights I've endured the pain and suffering of his windburn, my cheeks red from his hand.

Only I will know when I've had enough windburn. Only I will know when it's time to end my abusive relationship. Let me wear a scarf or a hat and cover myself from his blows as long as I can, but let me not stay a minute longer than necessary. I deserve to live without having to cover myself up all the time.

Let this day end with a breeze at my back and the gentle face of the sun shinning softly on me.

Dedicated to Cherrie and her two sons.

79. FRIENDS

What is a friend? When we are growing up, we believe we have many friends. There are those that play with us, those that ride bikes with us, those that walk to school with us, and those that skip down the street with us. And as we start learning the difference between friends and enemies, we find we have more acquaintances than friends. We still ride bikes and walk to school, and sometimes when no one else is around, we skip down the street.

Then we go to high school and our friends change again. Many do their own things, meet new friends, move away or sometimes die. All through my youth, I had many friends. Many were judgmental without knowing it. Only one or two accepted me 100 percent for who I was.

It wasn't until after I married, had children, divorced and started my life again that I actually thought about the meaning of friendship. A friend is someone you can trust, confide in, believe in, laugh with, cry with, dream with, and even as adults, skip down the street with. Today, I have only a select number of friends. I can choose who I call my "friend." I've learned the hard way, friends are difficult to find. Friends don't let friends down.

If you are in an abusive situation and need help, call a friend. Think before you start sharing your hurt, pain and life with just anyone. If you come to the conclusion that you have no friends, then maybe you need to get on the phone and talk with someone who understands what you are going through. Many hotlines, shelters, support groups and other resources have female volunteers and victims of domestic violence that can help you. One of those women may turn out to be a friend. You have nothing to lose, so make a friend today.

Dedicated to Roseanna. Without your help, strength and listening skills, I would not have come this far. You have given me so much that words cannot describe. I thank you and I love you from the bottom of my heart.

80. LISTENING

Listen to the echoes
There are echoes in my tunnel.
I hear voices that are only sounds.
When I listen to those voices I grow.
When I understand what I've heard, it gives me power.
If I act on that power, I am only the wiser.

We only hear what we want to hear. When our family or friends are telling us to leave him, telling us to call the cops, or telling us not to give him money because he'll only spend it on drugs or alcohol, we don't hear them. When we tell ourselves the same things, do we listen to our heads or to our hearts? The question should be, "do we put ourselves first or do we put our abuser first?"

First, we need to accept that we have to listen. It's only when we are ready to change that we start to hear we will benefit from keeping an open mind. It will help not to judge others who try to give advice. If you don't want advice, don't ask for it. If you don't want to hear someone's offering of help, don't listen. But remember asking for help is healthy. Asking for help is good. We all need outside help at one time or another in our lives. Find a support group where you can share your experiences as well as listen to others in similar situations.

Find a therapist who is a certified domestic violence specialist who you can listen to with an open mind. Listening is a gift that takes practice.

Dedicated to my cousin, Laura for her sense of humor, but most of all her friendship and love.

81. Fear

The fear that rises in my chest when he's putting the key in the front door is indescribable. My insides scream. How dare he have that much control over my feelings! He knows how much I fear him. When the door is unlocked, I pretend to be sleeping. I don't move. I don't open my eyes. I hardly breathe. I pray that he'll just pass out and not bother me.

When he does pass out...I am lucky. He mumbles to himself. He may call me names, but I refuse to respond. I won't let him get the best of me this time. I don't pull the covers off my face. He's so drunk that he finally goes to sleep. I take his boots off and cover him. Place a pillow under his head. Clean up the mess he made before he passed out.

When he doesn't pass out...He puts the lights on and pulls the covers off me. A sinister grin spreads across his face. He may get into bed with me. He may push me off the bed. He may yell at me. He may pull my hair or poke at my face. There are a 100 things he could possibly do to me.

Tonight he starts to tug at my hair. He tells me he saw a man that I went to high school with. I think, "big deal, a guy from high school." Well, that's not what my husband was thinking. He gets mad at me because this man knows me. My husband calls me a whore and tells me I'd better not be cheating on him. How absurd! I have one small child and I stayed home all night because we had no money and he's worrying about some guy from my high school.

My mouth stays shut tonight, but that doesn't matter. He hits me and kicks me out of bed. He makes me sleep on the couch. I wipe my bloody nose and cry myself to sleep. I dream of the day when I will be free from all of this.

Dedicated to Veronica and women so scared they don't dare go to sleep tonight.

82. ENOUGH IS ENOUGH

How long is long enough? What did it take for me to have enough abuse? I know each woman's limits and boundaries are different. We share the common thread of violence, but we each have ropes of different lengths.

My rope was fraying for many years. It took numerous black eyes, bloody lips, twisted arms, kicks, bruises, bites and lost clumps of hair to get to the end of my rope. It was not just the physical violence that took its toll on me — it was his mental, verbal, sexual and financial abuse, too.

Why did I allow him to degrade and humiliate me with his words? How many times did he call me a bitch, a whore, a pig and other shameful words in front of our friends, family and strangers? It did not matter to him where we were, he had to stay in control. He had to make me cry and show that he dominated me.

Enough was enough when I put my well-being ahead of his. Enough was enough when I allowed reality back into my life. Enough was enough when I told myself I could make it without him. Enough was enough when I set boundaries for myself and did not extend them for any reason. Enough was enough when I realized I loved myself. At first, it felt strange to love myself because I hadn't done it in so many years, but then it felt good. "Enough is enough" takes time, so give yourself the time you need to live without domestic violence.

Work towards your goals. Give yourself love and respect, because no one else can do it for you.

Dedicated to Janette, for sharing and for caring so openly.

83. HABITS

Have you ever changed your shampoo or your detergent? Painted your room? Went on a diet and lost weight? Tried a new toothpaste? Walked with your head up instead of looking at the ground? If you have done at least one of these things, then you have the ability to change.

These things probably seem minuscule. You're probably thinking so what, you've tried a new shampoo! Well, if you washed your hair and felt better, the new shampoo worked. If your clothes felt softer and smelled fresher, the detergent did its job. If you lost even five pounds, you felt better about your body. If your teeth looked whiter and your breath was fresher, the toothpaste did the trick. And if you walked with your head held high and someone smiled at you, you probably felt better...

you probably even smiled back.

If you have the power to change the little things then you can change the big ones as well. Change is inevitable. Change happens every day. Some days we don't notice the changes because we don't think about them. We may be too busy or too confused to notice subtle changes. We take our life habits for granted, like washing with the same soap in the same bathroom every day.

Today, think about the bigger changes you need to make, then start with the smallest one of all. Before you know it, you will change two or three things. After a while, you'll have no more room to count how many things you've changed in your life. Count the little things, count the big things, but make the changes you feel okay making. Take it day by day and change by change.

Dedicated to Brett, who felt he had no other choice left.

84. Say What You Mean

Do I say what I mean when I am trying to communicate with my abuser? Do I tell him I do not appreciate when he hits me, calls me degrading names, embarrasses me and mentally torments me? Do I speak with my head hanging low, looking at the ground, speaking so he can hardly hear me, telling him, "It's okay that you hit me, because I probably deserved it."

Believe me, I've looked down at the ground too often while talking to my abuser. I've studied every crack in the sidewalk. Sometimes he never heard my voice at all because I figured, "it wouldn't do any good to stand up for myself."

My life is different today. I do my best to say what I mean. Even though I am divorced from my abuser, I still do not like to look at him. And I still have days when I do not say what I mean. But as long as I try my best, I will grow and learn. That is all I can ask of myself.

At times, it's difficult for me to take a firm stand when I believe in something. It takes practice to boost my self-esteem, which was in the gutter for a long time. Today, allow me the courage to "say what I mean" instead of avoiding the subject or saying something I really do not want to say. Let me stand tall and be proud of what I have to say, because I am very important and what I have to say matters.

Dedicated to Robin from New Jersey who was killed by the hands that were supposed to protect her. May the Lord be with her mother and her three children.

May the lives she touched before her tragic death find peace on this day. And may all readers of this page take a moment of silence — for Robin and for themselves.

85. CRAWL, THEN WALK

All of us on this earth crawled before we walked. So in the face of domestic violence, allow me the strength and the courage to crawl. Sure, I wanted many times to run as fast as I could from of my abusive relationship, but it never happened that way. Many times I began to run and my abuser pushed me flat on my face.

Whether he pushed me down physically or mentally, he was the one in control. It wasn't until I realized I could only crawl out of my tunnel of violence by myself, without him, that I began my journey to freedom.

The old saying "you can run but you can't hide," can be changed to "you can crawl and you can be free." It took me a long time to fall victim to domestic violence and it will take me a while to rid myself of those memories. If I try to rush my situation, I may do myself more harm than good. At least allow me to crawl towards unlinking a link today.

Dedicated to Terri G. and all the nurses who have assisted me with my seminars, especially Gretchen W.

86. JUST HOLD ME

These past few weeks I've been running on fumes. My body has been mentally and physically drained. How much more can I handle without collapsing? I stare blankly into space, my head resting in my palms and I begin to rock back and forth for comfort. Right now, the only comfort I can get is from myself. When was the last time I was truly held and rocked by someone else? Can I remember being held by a man that said, "I'll never abuse you?"

If I don't have one person to trust enough to hold me while I cry, then allow me to wrap my arms around myself and hug tightly. If I need to release my pain and only my mirror image is staring back, give me the strength to tell it like it is.

My husband physically abuses me. That causes me pain and suffering. My husband mentally torments me daily. My husband tells me he will kill me if I leave him. My husband spits on me after he head butts my forehead. Damn, that hurts! Damn, he's a bastard! Damn, I'm really pissed off that I love this man and he hurts me. Damn...

Telling myself the truth shocks me. Maybe I need that shock to get back on track in my tunnel to recovery. God, I need your guidance. Please hold me today, because I am feeling alone. I know my loneliness will pass, but for today, I need your arms around me.

Dedicated to Karen S. for sharing her story with me. I enjoyed our lunch and your openness.

87. HE IS EMOTIONALLY IMPAIRED

Just as blood does not come from a stone, emotional support does not come from an unstable person. Whether I seek support from my mother, sister, aunt, cousin, friend, pastor, teacher, a co-worker or from the abuser himself, if those I choose are unable to fulfill my needs, then I must travel a new path.

Frustrated as you may feel, remember unhealthy people give unhealthy support. If you really think about it, a person that inflicts mental, physical, verbal and/or sexual abuse on someone is outright unhealthy. An abusive person abuses because he is powerless over his own emotions. If he is powerless over himself, then he probably can't give you the emotional support you deserve.

Today, look to only those you know are emotionally stable. The more emotionally healthy people you have around you, the healthier you become. Good things come to those who allow goodness into their lives.

Dedicated to Ken D. for making a difference in the lives of domestic violence victims.

88. Give your Child a Chance Today

Today is a day to give your child the chance he or she deserves. After all, aren't we all deserving of such a chance? Today is a day to consider your child's feelings, pain, suffering, powerlessness, and loneliness caused by family violence. Consider what he or she is going through. Embrace your child. Embrace the love he or she has for you. Embrace the trust he or she puts in you. Embrace your child as you did the first time you held him or her in your arms—your little miracle. Embrace them today, for now *you* can be their miracle. You have the power to get yourself and your child to a safe place if you choose to do so. You and your child deserve a safe environment. You both deserve to be free from domestic violence.

It is never too late to give that chance to your child. No matter what age he or she is, there is help where there is hope. The statistics show that 74 percent of children who witness violence in their homes have a greater chance of committing crimes against people. Numbers like that scream loud and clear. It's time for parents in abusive relationships to consider their child's future.

Dedicated to all children who witness family violence.

89. Labeled Like a Can

Outsiders. Family members. Friends. Law enforcement officials. Neighbors. The people who view my abusive relationship from the outside of my prison judge me along with my abuser. They do this without realizing the harm they cause. The harm is done when a victim of domestic violence hears others ridiculing her for tolerating the abuse. She takes the blame. She sees fingers pointing in her direction. She starts to believe that the abuse she endures is her own fault. She feels abused all over again.

Now you cannot stop the public from voicing their opinions. It is their Constitutional right. But what you can do is educate them as best you can about domestic violence. You have an opportunity to express your opinions about domestic violence, stand proud and allow your beliefs to be heard. State your convictions with dignity. Do not raise your voice or shout, but say what you have to say. Let others know that no woman is at fault for being abused. Tell them that battered women have the same rights they do. Grant me this day to be heard.

Dedicated to Kimberley, Leigh and Mellony for their support, compassion and understanding.

90. A Story Too Painful to Hear

As I was doing research for this book, I came across a question and answer sheet for professionals. The reason employees do not approach a co-worker they believe is being abused is because they fear her story will be too painful to hear.

The fear of hearing my own painful story keeps me from talking to others about my abusive situation. Until this moment, I could not find the words to express why I had difficulty sharing my experiences. Just as others are afraid to hear domestic violence stories, I am afraid to tell mine because I'll have to hear it, too.

Hear no more the words "you are lying about your abuse." Hear no more the words "you must be provoking him to hurt you." Today, hear yourself cry for your pain and suffering. Hear your own words describing your torment and sadness. Don't be alone anymore. Tell your story to a trusting therapist, friend, or support group as soon as you feel comfortable doing so. If you cannot share your pain today, it is all right. Just knowing that one day you can and will be heard.

Dedicated to my three sisters and two brothers that stood by my side during many difficult times.

91. Consequences When You Leave

After the police escorted my abuser out of our home, my abuser's "paybacks" were almost worse than the violence he had inflicted on me day after day for so long. For example, he threw a brick through my window. He broke the mirrors on my car. He chased me in a parking lot. He harassed me by telephone more than 100 times a day. He mentally and verbally abused me in public. Once, my estranged husband even entered my home by force and ripped my shirt off and called me disgusting names in front of our children.

Am I frightening you into thinking twice about leaving your abuser? That's not my intention. For your sake, I hope you are a bit frightened. But I also share the experiences I had when I left so you will remember not to let your guard down.

Women who leave their abusive partners are at a higher risk of physical and mental torment than those who remain in their abusive situations. These are the facts. Take them or leave them today, but sooner or later please take them and act on them.

Today, get back to the reality of your circumstances. If you let your guard down today, find the strength to pick it back up tomorrow. Walk not in fear, but in caution.

Dedicated to the reader of this page. May it help you unchain enough links to make a light strong enough to lead you through your tunnel.

92. SORROW

How much sorrow do I feel when I think about what I lost by living a life of violence and fear? I lived a life of intimidation. I lived a life of lies. My hopes and dreams for a "happily ever after" marriage are gone. My dreams of building a life with the person I chose as my husband are broken. Hopes once shared with a partner no longer exist, yet they still pierce my flesh when I remember them. I lost, and I lost big.

If I linger on the word "sorrow," it depresses me and brings tears to my eyes. Sorrow is what I feel today. Grief binds me with its emotions. It's a grief so forceful, it whips up a whirlwind around me. I cry. I am sad.

I believe all women that are dominated and abused by a person they wanted to share hopes and their dreams with have the same type of sorrow. When other women in my battered women's group discuss their own anguish over the loss of the dreams they built with someone they love or once loved, my own feelings of deprivation flood my heart. After all, I too was deprived of what I believed was rightfully mine.

Allow me this day to work through my feelings of loss. If I can mourn today knowing that when I wake up tomorrow these feelings of sadness will be a little less painful, give me this day to weep.

Dedicated to Wilma and her two children for what they face each day from the man that is supposed to love them.

93. To Feel Like a Woman

There were many years when I never felt like a "real woman." For years, I wore loose clothing to prevent others from seeing the shape of my body. I went years without being allowed to wear makeup or fix my hair. I didn't have female friends for years. I endured years of criticism. During these years, I couldn't even show interest in activities outside my home. I wasn't allowed to act like a woman, how could I possibly feel like one?

Today, let me make a bold statement: "I am a strong-willed woman surviving the toughest of circumstances." My own definition of the word woman comes from within myself. If I can practice loving myself on this day, then maybe I can begin to feel like a woman again.

If confidence shines from inside of me, allow me to smile in a crowded room and walk like I'm the sexiest, most beautiful woman alive. That's how I want to feel on this day.

Dedicated to all the Prudential employees that have supported my efforts of educating people about the epidemic of domestic violence.

94. THE MISSING SHOES

After the birth of my third child, I had to go back to work. I was back at work in just six weeks and my work clothes and accessories were back in use. One day, I went into my closet to put on a pair of heels, only to discover one shoe was missing from every pair. That left me with two thoughts: First I thought my husband had gotten rid of one shoe to every pair so I couldn't wear them. And second I thought what was I going to wear to a job that required me to dress like a businesswoman?

After working all day in my sneakers, I asked my husband why he took my shoes. His response was, "only sluts wear heels." This comment wasn't out of the ordinary to me. It was typical behavior of him. I accepted his actions and the verbal abuse, just like any other day. I didn't know it then, but throwing away one shoe from every pair was his way to get back some of the control he had lost when I began working again.

As with almost all domestic violence relationships, control and power are the two key elements that make a batterer tick. If I am able to acknowledge that his behavior is unacceptable, I can learn to accept the reality of my situation.

Dedicated to Esta, Carla, Monica, Janet, Marissa, Vilma, Patti, Suzie, Lisa, Darrell, Debbie, Leni, Sue, Kevin, Kelly, Doris, Leah, Donna, Janet, Mojgan, Josephine, Irene, Yolanda, Christina, Jacquelyn, Valerie, Ellen, Beckie, Paulette, Marie and the rest of the family at the Family Violence Prevention Fund.

95. Dates Filled With Pain

Birthdays, anniversaries, holidays, deaths, vacations, and the days I was beaten. These dates will stay in the back of my mind forever. Just as I remember the birth of my sons, I will always remember the days of my "black and blues."

The Superbowl reminds me of unhappiness. It was a time of bruises and stitches. It brought embarrassment, fear, doubt, sadness, loneliness and unnecessary suffering. It symbolized a day to celebrate and a day to mourn. I remember sitting in the hospital emergency waiting room crying and struggling to compose myself. I remember telling my dad that I could not press charges against my husband for beating me.

It's been a long road and many Superbowls have passed since then. I'm wiser, but I'm still learning and growing. I remember those dates, but I don't dwell on them—there's not enough time in each day.

Let me enjoy every day, for each one is a gift. Let me make this date a happy memory.

Dedicated to Margarita in New York for her courage and strength.

96. It's His Birthday and I'll Cry if I Want To

Yes, it is the day my abusive husband entered this world. This day is not for celebration, but for mourning. I choose this day to mourn the loss of the hopes and dreams I once shared with my batterer. I mourn, not to get depressed and angry, but to learn to heal the open wounds of my abusive years. I mourn the loss of the laughter we once shared together. I mourn the days we enjoyed each other's company. And I mourn the biggest loss of all—the loss of my love for him. He's become an individual I can only refer to as "him." I can't call him beloved husband, trusted partner or soul-mate.

Let me mourn my personal losses on this day. Let me mourn in my own way, and in my own time, but let me not consume myself with this mourning. For if I can weep and feel sadness today, then my healing process is underway. In the healing process, I grow wiser about this epidemic called "domestic violence." That's what this book is all about—educating myself and others about the true meaning of domestic violence.

Dedicated to Jane and Jim for their friendship. They are two of the world's best people.

97. It's Not How Far You Have to Go, It's How Far You've Come

No one knows better then you all the struggles, hardships, sacrifices and difficult choices you've had to endure. Unfortunately, many of the people you wish to share your experiences with may never fully understand how you feel or what you've really been through.

As for my own sacrifices, they remain embedded in my soul, but I am not trapped by them. As my inner strength flourishes each day, the realization of how far I've actually come makes me proud to be who I am. For today, I know who I am, and it no longer matters how far I have to go. As long as I make it a priority to move forward in my recovery, I will reach my tunnel's light.

Sometimes, measuring your own growth is difficult. Take this day to know you have made at least one step in your recovery — picking up this self-help book and reading it. May the coming days be filled with progress. May you walk with your head held high, your self-esteem improved and your understanding of domestic violence broader. May your Higher Power be with you always. Stay strong, stay focused and keep walking toward your tunnel's light. You are not alone.

Dedicated to Laura C. and our newfound friendship.

98. Education

If I make one small step today, let me educate myself about what resources are available to me.

If every hour, over 400 American women are abused, why should I believe that I am alone? If domestic violence kills thousands of women and children each year, will I be the next murder victim?

Eighty percent of Americans say they would do something to help reduce domestic violence if they knew what to do. Let me take today to learn how I can help myself. First, I'll ask my Higher Power to give me the courage to call a hotline, shelter or community resource center. If I can't get to a phone, let me take a ride or walk to a bookstore to read about women in abusive situations. Or let me check the yellow pages for a support group in my town.

By taking this first step, I have accepted that I am not alone, and that there is help available.

Dedicated to Mildred, Ron, George, Kristen, Terri, Beverly, Tom, Diane, Susan, Deb, Christine and the hundreds of other people who have attended my domestic violence workshops.

99. Anxiety and Panic

So many of us suffer anxiety and panic attacks. I know first-hand how scary and humiliating these attacks can be. I suffer from them.

It's hard to go through your daily routine without getting stressed. It's even harder when violence, fear, uncertainty, looking over your shoulder and flashbacks are part of that routine. All of these things increase my daily struggles, and some days, panic attacks just kick in without warning.

Some of the symptoms are:

- Rocking back and forth to comfort yourself.
- Feeling like you're going to die.
- Being ashamed to take medication.
- Feeling like a failure.
- Keeping busy, so you don't have to sit down.
- Going to sleep so your mind doesn't wonder.
- Being unable to cry or crying too much.

These are just a few of the things that happen to me when I'm in anxiety or panic mode. It's mostly as a result of living in constant fear for so long that the concept of a "normal" life is strange to me.

Today, give me the power to know that I'll be OK. Just for today, allow me to go through my daily routine without being afraid.

Dedicated to Tammy H. for caring about those who are suffering from this epidemic.

100. To Be Free

Freedom. What a powerful word. It's a word that can make or break a person.

Freedom is a choice for all women in abusive situations. We have the choice to stay, and we have the choice to leave. Freedom may not be about leaving your situation. It may mean getting a part-time job, or attending a support group. Freedom may be a walk in the park for just a few minutes, or using the telephone without being harassed.

A few years ago, those things meant freedom to me, but today, freedom means having the power to walk out of my house without being afraid. It means staying late at work and not worrying about what's in store for me when I get home. Freedom means being able to wear white clothes and put on make-up. It's about having friends and knowing what my likes and dislikes are. It means being the "queen of my castle."

Freedom. One word, so many meanings.

As I look back to 1984, I see myself as a young girl, unsure of so many things. I see a fifteen year old who had her freedom stolen from her in the blink of an eye, yet it took over a decade to reclaim that freedom.

In the 17 years that have passed since my first physical assault by my former husband, I've grown tremendously as a human being, mother, sister, girlfriend, employee, aunt, cousin, and woman.

Not only because of what abuse I've endured, but by who has entered my life. And because of that, I'm free to chose whomever I want to be a part of my world. I'm free to stand up for myself. Free to buy what clothes I like. Free to be spontaneous. Free to laugh, cry, look at those around me and not feel ashamed of who I am. I'm free to talk to men and use the phone without it being bashed on my head. I'm finally free to leave my door unlocked.

I'm free to wear make-up, cut my hair and have my nails done. I'm free to say what's going on in my life without feeling guilty. I'm free to not watch the door all night. I'm free to go to bed in peace. I'm free to hug my children knowing that I probably saved their lives.

I'm free to go to therapy and talk with others about how domestic violence must not be kept silent. Best of all—I'm just plain free.

Dedicated to you and your freedom.

HELPING YOURSELF OR A LOVED ONE

— Did you know that domestic violence is a crime?

— Did you know that by talking to a victim without judging is one of the best things you could do to help?

— Did you ever think that a simple hug could mean so much to the one receiving it?

— Have you ever thought about volunteering at a battered women's shelter or community center?

— Can you look at yourself in the mirror and like who's starring back? If so, list why you like that person. If you don't like what you see, ask yourself why not and take one step toward liking yourself.

— Did you realize you're not a failure if you ask for help?

— Do you think you can hide your abuse from your children? 80% to 90% of children living in homes where there is domestic violence know what's going on.

— Can you talk to someone you trust about the abuse? 57% of battered women do not discuss their incidents with anyone.

You Are Not Alone

— Four million women a year are battered by an intimate partner. That's over 400 an hour!

— Rape occurs in 50% of abusive relationships on a regular basis.

— 40% of teenage girls (14-17) know someone their age who has been hit or beaten by a boyfriend.

— Three out of five rapes happen before age 18.

— Domestic violence affects rich, poor and middle class women. It destroys families, friendships, gets victims fired from their jobs and devastates children for life.

— 42% of murdered women are killed by an intimate male partner.

— $3-5 billion is lost by businesses each year as a direct result of domestic violence.

— Over 3 million children are subject to witness partner violence each year.

You Are Not Alone

— 30% of Americans say they know a woman who has been physically abused by her husband or boyfriend.

— 18% of women reported they had been raped and/or physically assaulted since age 18.

— 80% of women who are stalked by their current or former intimate partner are physically assaulted by that partner and 30% are sexually assaulted.

— 45% of female victims of domestic violence lived in a home with children under the age of 12.

— 1/4 of all suicide attempts are by battered women.

— There are an estimated 13,000 acts of violence against women at work each year by their partners.

— 74% of employed battered women experience harassment at work by abusive partners, either in person or on the telephone.

— 95% of women murdered by a current or former male partner were stalked prior to their death.

ORGANIZATIONS

Doorways to Freedom
P.O. Box 403, Kearny, NJ 07032-0403
(201) 998-5929

Family Violence Prevention Fund
383 Rhode Island Street #304
San Francisco, CA 94103-5133
(415) 252-8900

Atlantic County Women's Center — VIP
PO Box 311 Northfield, NJ 08225

Burlington County Providence House
PO Box 496 Willingboro, NJ 08046

Cumberland County Women's Center
PO Box 921 Vineland, NJ 08362

The Safe House
PO Box 1887 Bloomfield, NJ 07003

Hunterdon County Women's Crisis Svc.
47 E. Main Street Flemington, NJ 08822

ORGANIZATIONS

Batterers Services — Family Growth Ctr
39 N. Clinton Ave Trenton, NJ 08607

Batterers Services — Family Violence Program
288 Rues Lane East Brunswick, NJ 08816

Jersey Battered Women's Svc Inc (JBWS)
PO Box 363 Morris Plains, NJ 07950

Rape Crisis Program
1027 Madison Avenue Paterson, NJ 07513

Women Rising (formerly YWCA of Hudson County)
270 Fairmount Ave Jersey City, NJ 07306

Salem County Women's Services
PO Box 125 Salem, NJ 08079

Somerset County — Resource Center for
Women & Their Families
427 Homestead Road Belle Mead, NJ 08502

Bergen County — Shelter Our Sisters
PO Box 217 Hackensack, NJ 07602

ORGANIZATIONS

Alternatives to Domestic Violence
21 Main Street Room 111 West Hackensack, NJ 07601

Camden County YWCA/Solace
PO Box 1309 Blackwood, NJ 08102

Cape May County CARA Inc.
PO Box 774 Cape May Court House, NJ 08210

Essex County Family Violence Program
755 South Orange Ave Newark, NJ 07106

Outreach PEACE Center
3 Royal Avenue Livingston, NJ 07039

National Council of Jewish Women
513 W. Mt. Pleasant Ave Suite 325 Livingston, NJ 07039

Gloucester County—People Against Spouse Abuse
PO Box 755 Glassboro, NJ 08028

Mercer County—Womenspace, Inc.
1212 Stuyvesant Ave Trenton, NJ 08618

ORGANIZATIONS

Outreach
1860 Brunswick Ave Lawrenceville, NJ 08648

Middlesex County — Women Aware Inc.
PO Box 312 New Brunswick, NJ 08903

Outreach
96 Paterson Street New Brunswick, NJ 08901

Batterers Services — Challenge Program
312 Amboy Ave Metuchen, NJ 08873

The Women's Ctr of Monmouth County
One Bethany Road, Bldg #3 Suite 42 Hazlet, NJ 07730

Ocean County Providence House
PO Box 104 Toms River, NJ 08754

Passaic County Women's Center
Domestic Violence Program
PO Box 244 Paterson, NJ 07513

Sussex County Domestic Violence Svc
PO Box 805 Newton, NJ 07860

ORGANIZATIONS

Batterers Svc—Mental Health Assoc
15 Alden Street Cranford, NJ 07016

Coalition Annex Office
2614 Whitehorse-Hamilton Sq Rd Trenton, NJ 08690-2718

Batterers Services DECIDE Program
35 High Street Newton, NJ 07860

Warren County—Domestic Abuse & Rape Crisis Center
(DARCC) PO Box 423 Belvidere, NJ 07823

Office on the Prevention of Violence Against Women
NJ Division PO Box 801 Trenton, NJ 08625

American Bar Association Commission
on Domestic Violence
740 15th N.W., 9th Floor Washington, D.C. 20005-1009

Natl Clearinghouse: Marital & Date Rape
2325 Oak Street Berkely, CA 9408

Women's Rights Info Center
108 West Palisade Ave Englewood, NJ 07631

ORGANIZATIONS

Alabama Coalition Against Violence
PO Box 4762 Montgomery, AL 36010 (205) 832-4842

Alaska Network on Domestic Violence and Sexual
Assault 130 Seward Street Room 501 Juneau, AK 99801

AZ Coalition Against Domestic Violence
100 West Camelback, #109 Phoenix, AZ 85013
(800) 782-6400

AR Coalition Against Violence to Women & Children
7509 Cantrell Road, Suite 213 Little Rock, AR 72207

CA Alliance Against Domestic Violence
Marin Abused Women's Services
1717-5th Ave San Rafael, CA 94901 (415) 457-2464

Southern CA Coalition Against Domestic Violence
PO Box 5036 Santa Monica, CA 90405

Colorado Domestic Violence Coalition
PO Box 18902 Denver, CO 80218 (303) 573-9018

ORGANIZATIONS

Connecticut Coalition Against Violence
135 Broad Street Hartford, CT 06105 (203) 524-5890

Florida Coalition Against Violence
PO Box 5099 Gainsville, FL 32602

Georgia Advocates for Battered Women
250 Georgia Ave, SE Suite 308 Atlanta, GA 30312
(404) 524-3847

Hawaii State Committee on Family Violence
2500 Pali Highway Honolulu, HI 96817 (808) 595-3900

Idaho Coalition Against Sexual and Domestic Violence
200 North 4th Street, Suite 10-K Boise, ID 83702

IL Coalition Against Domestic Violence
937 South Fourth Street Springfield, IL 62703
(217) 789-2830

Indiana Coalition Against Violence Inc.
622 West 10th Street Anderson, IN 46016

ORGANIZATIONS

IA Coalition Against Domestic Violence
Lucas State Office Building, 1st Floor
Des Moines, IA 50319 (515) 281-7284

KS Coalition Against Sexual & Domestic Violence
820 SE Quincy, Suite 416B Topeka, KS 66612
(913) 232-9784

KY Domestic Violence Association
PO Box 356 Frankfort, KY 40602 (502) 875-4132

LA Coalition Against Domestic Violence
PO Box 303 Hammond, LA 70404 (504) 542-4446

Maine Coalition for Family Crisis Svc
359 Main Street Bangor, ME 04402

MD Network Against Domestic Violence
11501 Georgia Ave., Suite 403
Silver Spring, MD 20902 (301) 942-0900

ORGANIZATIONS

Massachusetts Coalition of Battered Women Services
210 Commercial St., 3rd Floor Boston, MA 02109

MI Coalition Against Domestic Violence
PO Box 16009 Lansing, MI 48901 (517) 484-2924

MN Coalition for Battered Women
1619 Dayton Ave., Suite 303
St. Paul, MN 55104 (612) 646-6177

MS Coalition Against Domestic Violence
PO Box 4703 Jackson, MS 39296-4703 (601) 981-9196

MT Coalition Against Domestic Violence
1236 North 28th Street Billings, MT 59101 (406) 245-7990

NE Domestic Violence Sexual Assault Coalition
315 South 19th Street Suite 18
Lincoln, NE 68508-2253 (402) 476-6256

NV Network Against Domestic Violence
2100 Capurro Way Suite E
Sparks, NV 89431 (702) 358-1171

ORGANIZATIONS

NH Coalition
Against Domestic Violence & Sexual Assault
PO Box 353 Concord, NH 03302-0353 (603) 224-8893

NJ Coalition for Battered Women
2620 Whitehorse-Hamilton Sq Rd
Trenton, NJ 08690-2718 (609) 584-8107

NM Coalition Against Domestic Violence
2329 Wisconsin NE, Suite F
Albuquerque, NM 87110 (505) 296-7876

NY Coalition Against Domestic Violence
The Women's Building
79 Central Avenue Albany, NY 12206 (800) 942-6906

NC Coalition Against Domestic Violence
PO Box 51875 Durham, NC 27717-1875 (919) 956-9124

ND Council on Abused Women's Svc
418 East Rosser Avenue, Suite 320
Bismark, ND 58501 (701) 255-6240

ORGANIZATIONS

Ohio Domestic Violence Network
4041 North High Street #101
Columbus, OH 43214 (800) 934-9840

National Coalition Against Domestic Violence (NCADV)
P.O. Box 18749 Denver, CO 80218

Statewide California Coalition for Battered Women
3711 Long Beach Blvd., Suite 718
Long Beach, CA 90807

Girls Incorporated National Resources Center
441 West Michigan Street
Indianapolis, IN 46202
www.girlsinc.org

The Empower Program
1312 8th Street, NW
Washington, DC 20001
www.empowered.org

National Domestic Violence Hotline 1-800-799-SAFE

INTERNET RESOURCES

American Bar Association
www.abanet.org

Bureau of Justice Statistics, U.S. Department of Justice
www.ojp.usdoj.gov

Center for Disease Control and Prevention
www.cdc.gov

The Empower Program
www.empowered.org

The Family Violence Prevention Fund
www.fvpf.org

Girls Incorporated National Resource Center
www.girlsinc.org

Los Angeles Commission on Assaults Against Women
in Touch with Teens Program
www.lacaaw.org

www.menovercomingviolence.org

Men's Rape Prevention Project
www.mrppc.org

National Center for Victims of Crime
www.ncvc.org

INTERNET RESOURCES

National Coalition Against Domestic Violence/
Teen Dating Violence Project
www.ncadv.org

National Coalition Against Sexual Assault
www.ncasa.org

R.A.I.N.N. (Rape Abuse Incest National Network)
www.rain.org

Security on Campus
www.securityoncampus.org

Stalked (stories and support)
www.francieweb.com/stalked

State Stalking Laws
www.nvc.org/law/statestk.htm

Victim Services Network
www.victimservices.org

The Whole Family Center
www.wholefamily.com

Workplace Violence Research Institute
www.noworkviolence.com

Index of Subjects

INDEX OF SUBJECTS